AF870274

ASSOCIATION OF ACADEMIC HEALTH CENTERS

Global Dimensions of Domestic Health Issues

Marian Osterweis
Denise E. Holmes
Editors

The Association of Academic Health Centers is dedicated to improving the health of the people by advancing the leadership of academic health centers in health professions education, biomedical and health services research, and health care delivery.

The AHC is a national, non-profit organization representing more than 100 institutional members in the United States that are the health complexes of the nation's major universities. Academic health centers consist of an allopathic or osteopathic school of medicine, at least one other health professions school or program, and one or more teaching hospitals.

The views expressed in this book are those of its authors and do not necessarily represent the views of the Board of Directors of the Association of Academic Health Centers or its membership at large.

This publication was supported by grants from Pfizer, Inc., the Burroughs Wellcome Fund, and the Kaludis Consulting Group.

Printed in the United States of America

ISBN 1-879694-17-4

Copies of this book are available from:
Association of Academic Health Centers
1400 16th Street, N.W., Suite 720
Washington, D.C. 20036
Telephone: 202-265-9600
Facsimile: 202-265-7514
www.ahcnet.org
Price: US$25.00 (plus US$5.00 shipping & handling)

Design and production: Fletcher Design, Washington, DC

Table of Contents

Contributors

Jo Ivey Boufford, MD, Dean of the Robert F. Wagner Graduate School of Public Service at New York University, was the U.S. representative on the executive board of the World Health Organization. She also served as the U.S. Department of Health and Human Services' principal deputy assistant secretary for health.

Nils Daulaire, MD, MPH, is president and CEO of the Global Health Council and has represented the United States at the last five World Health Organization assemblies. As the Clinton Administration's senior international health expert, he served as the lead health negotiator at the Cairo International Conference on Population and Development, the Beijing World Conference on Women, and the Rome World Food Summit.

James M. Hughes, MD, FACP, is director of the National Center for Infectious Diseases at the Centers for Disease Control and Prevention. He also serves as an assistant surgeon general in the U.S. Public Health Service and is a fellow of the American College of Physicians and the Infectious Disease Society of America.

Robert J. Levine, MD, FACP, is professor of medicine and lecturer in pharmacology at the Yale University School of Medicine. He chairs international committees on the ethics of biomedical research for the United Nations, the World Medical Association, and the Council of International Organizations of Medical Sciences.

Theodore R. Marmor, PhD, a professor of public policy and management and political science at the Yale School of Management in New Haven, is also the director of The Robert Wood Johnson Foundation's postdoctoral program in social science and health policy. He has been a faculty member at the Universities of Chicago, Minnesota, and Wisconsin.

Virginia D. McGill is director of the Institute for Latin American Concern (ILAC) at Creighton University, where she is the founder and director of ILAC's physical therapy and occupational therapy programs. She also is founder of the university's Dublin Service Corps in Ireland and cofounder of the Semestre Dominicano programs.

George M. Milne, Jr., PhD, is senior vice president of Pfizer, Inc., where he also serves as president of the Central Research Division. He has held a variety of prominent positions in immunology, infectious diseases, and research and development and serves on numerous health-related corporate and association boards.

Joel J. Nobel, MD, is president of ECRI, a nonprofit, nongovernmental organization conducting health services research. For twelve years, Dr. Nobel has directed the ECRI-World Health Organization Collaborating Center. He is also a diplomate of the National Board of Medical Examiners.

Richard L. O'Brien, MD, is professor of medicine at Creighton University. He recently retired as vice president for health sciences at the university, where he also served as dean of the School of Medicine. He has served on the boards of the Association of Academic Health Centers, the Association of American Cancer Institutes, and the California Division of the American Cancer Society.

John Pakutka is president of The Crescent Group, LLC, a health care management/information technology consulting firm founded in 1998.

Pablo A. Pulido, MD, FACP, is founder and former director of the Centro Medico Docente La Trinidad, in Caracas, Venezuela, where he also serves as president of the medical center's investment firm, Inversora. Before joining the Centro Medico, Dr. Pulido served as Venezuela's minister of health and social welfare.

Vulimiri Ramalingaswami, MD, DPhil, is president of India's National Institute of Immunology, as well as India's National Research Professor and Professor Emeritus at the All India Institute of Medical Sciences. He served as a special advisor to the United Nations Children's Fund, secretary-general for the International Conference on Nutrition, and director-general for the Indian Council of Medical Research.

David Satcher, MD, PhD, is the sixteenth surgeon general of the United States and only the second person in U.S. history to simultaneously hold the positions of surgeon general and assistant secretary for health. Prior to his appointment, Dr. Satcher was director of the Centers for Disease Control and Prevention.

Louis W. Sullivan, MD, is president of the Morehouse School of Medicine. Prior to this appointment, Dr. Sullivan was the secretary of health and human services. A former chairman of the board of the Association of Academic Health Centers, he currently serves on numerous corporate and association boards.

Steven J. Thompson, MBA, is vice dean for administration at the Johns Hopkins University School of Medicine. Mr. Thompson also is CEO of both Johns Hopkins International, LLC, and Johns Hopkins Singapore. He has held administrative posts in Johns Hopkins' departments of anesthesiology, surgery, and transplantation.

Preface

HOW RAPIDLY OUR PLANET, NOT TO MENTION THE professional worlds in which clinicians, health professions educators, researchers, administrators and policy makers operate, is shrinking. U.S.-based academic health centers today recruit students, faculty, and researchers from other lands and conduct extensive research and outreach delivery efforts abroad. Even more striking are the health implications of events and circumstances in other nations that increasingly—and sometimes dramatically—affect us here at home.

Globalization amounts to far more than an economic phenomenon. Politics, policies, and technology have contributed to the disregard and erosion of national borders so that health risks and health care now know no boundaries. *Global Dimensions of Domestic Health Issues,* a set of papers presented at the 1999 annual meeting of the Association of Academic Health Centers (AHC), takes a broad view of those health issues, transcending delivery of care to encompass health professions education, research, and policies that affect health. Thus, in this volume, distinguished speakers from the United States and abroad proffer answers to thorny questions of the age: What role can academic institutions play in setting the global agenda for health and mitigating health problems? Although cost, quality, and access are common problems around the world, how do national circumstances—history, resources, and culture—contribute to distinctive approaches to health care? What are some of the practical and ethical issues that arise in the course of technology development and multinational clinical trials? What are the implications of multinational credentialing for our educational institutions, for health workforce migration, and hence for access to health care?

The reader will find some responsive proposals and many words of wisdom in this volume. Taking a broad view of the work yet to be accomplished, U.S. Surgeon General and Assistant Secretary for Health David Satcher harkens back to the Declaration of Alma-Ata in advancing our nation's commitment to working as part of a global community to enhance global health status. In examining the global health agenda, Jo Ivey Boufford of New York University lauds the World Health Organization as a champion of global health outreach, health promotion, and disease prevention. Robert Levine of Yale University asserts that the Declaration of Helsinki has lost its force, and proffers an alternative international standard that he deems sufficiently flexible.

Two authors with remarkable breadth of experience in global health also offered sage counsel. Nils Daulaire of the Global Health Council, who received the John P. McGovern Award at the annual meeting, share a sweeping vision of national security, raising the specter of unanticipated threats likely to arise in the near future because of poverty, poor health and politics. Vulimiri Ramalingaswami, India's National Research Professor, who received the John R. Hogness Award also at our conference, caution about the need for intertwining scientific knowledge and action, offering examples of some of the ills produced by failure to put together such a mix.

Other papers remind the reader that crisis and opportunity often walk hand in hand. Joel Nobel of ECRI laments the problem of distortion in academic research and shares a vignette to illustrate some of the unusual challenges of technology assessment. Louis Sullivan of Morehouse School of Medicine and Virginia McGill of Creighton University describe their institutions' highly effective outreach efforts in South Africa and the Dominican Republic, respectively. James Hughes of the Centers for Disease Control and Prevention recites aspects of public health preparedness in response to the current threat of bioterrorism. George Milne of Pfizer and Steven Thompson of Johns Hopkins International describe some of their corporations' work to enhance health care delivery and health status abroad through creative use of new drugs, technologies, and health care systems.

Finally, several papers address the value of and mechanisms for international exchange. Pablo Pulido of the Pan-American Federation of Associations of Medical Schools hails the potential of distance learning as an inter-American educational tool. Richard O'Brien of Creighton University weighs the merit of international standards of professional competence. Theodore Marmor of Yale University and John Pakutka of The Crescent Group emphasize that learning about another's experience is not necessarily equivalent to learning from that experience.

Global Dimensions of Domestic Health Issues represents the first major product of AHC's recently established Division of Global Health. The Division of Global Health will continue to address the associated challenges in this realm. Through its strategic collaborations with other organizations, the AHC hopes to enhance the ability of academic health centers to work effectively to improve health and health policies worldwide.

We thank our extraordinary authors for their insightful and provocative words. The AHC also expresses its sincere gratitude to Pfizer, Inc., the Burroughs Wellcome Fund, and the Kaludis Consulting Group for their generous support of the meeting and this publication. Finally, we appreciate the editorial assistance provided by Ann M. Thompson of AMT Communications, the graphic design skill of Richard Fletcher of Fletcher Design, the final editorial reading performed by Shirley Sirota Rosenberg of SSR, Incorporated, and the manuscript production assistance provided by Hope Neely.

Marian Osterweis, Ph.D.
Executive Vice President and
Director, Division of Global Health

Denise E. Holmes, J.D., M.P.H.
Director, AHC/HRSA Center for Interdisciplinary,
Community-Based Learning and
Liaison to the American International Health Alliance

Association of Academic Health Centers

ENHANCING HEALTH CARE

1. Global Health: The Key to Security at Home and Abroad

NILS DAULAIRE

MOST OF US IN THE HEALTH PROFESSIONS HAVE A simple response to the question of why we engage in global health: We do it because it is right to help those who are sick and in need, and because it is at the heart of our calling as health professionals. It is why I devoted two decades to working as a doctor serving the health needs of people in far-flung corners of the world. It is why many faculty members take leaves and sabbaticals to help hurricane victims in Honduras or AIDS-affected communities in South Africa or maternal and child health clinics in India. Global health gives us an opportunity to give something back in exchange for all we have been given.

However, as noble as these moral and humanitarian motives may be, the fact is that in our changing world, concern with world global health is more than an ethical issue; it is fast emerging as a fundamental national interest for the United States. There is no security without world health. As

Note: This paper is based on the John P. McGovern Award Lecture presented by the author at the 1999 annual meeting of the Association of Academic Health Centers.

policy makers and world leaders come to recognize this precept, health care practitioners have an increasingly important role to play in promoting world health.

REDEFINING NATIONAL SECURITY

Before one maintains that something is vital to U.S. national security, it is essential to make a clear and compelling case based upon objective analysis rather than self-interest. No doubt the Hog Farmers Association thinks that pork belly futures are vital to U.S. foreign policy. Foreign policy exists for two clearly delineated purposes, and two purposes only: to protect vital national interests and to project core national values.

How do we define national security, and how have the United States security interests changed over the past half-century? In a world of nation-states separated by history, culture, warfare, and hostility, security traditionally has been defined in terms of armed conflict. The concept of protecting national security traditionally implied the ability to repel attacks from, or carry out attacks against, other hostile nation-states. Diplomacy, termed most famously as "war by other means," initially was developed as an adjunct to military efforts. An even better description comes from Will Rogers, who said, "Diplomacy is the art of saying, 'Nice Doggy' until you can find a rock."

When seen in this context, the appropriate people at the table for a discussion of national security were generals and diplomats. They were indeed the people who led U.S. foreign policy in the several decades following World War II. It is notable that, even among them, a broader vision sometimes emerged. After all, George Marshall, father of the Marshall Plan, was both a military general and secretary of state. The high watermark of the conflict-oriented view of national security and U.S. foreign policy came with the ascendance of Henry Kissinger, the epitome of a strategic thinker, whose entire focus was upon resolving conflicts.

However, the 1970s and 1980s were a time of profound change around the world and in the United States. As a consequence, our thinking about the parameters of national security was forced to change. To a remarkable extent, the United States had been a self-contained economy and society;

now the United States suddenly faced the imposing recognition of a world reality, namely, globalization is the flow of information, goods, capital, and people across political and geographic boundaries.

It was not a new force in the 1970s and 80s; in fact, the history of humankind is a history of progressive globalization from the time of the first migrations across the Bering Strait. What was new was the rapidly accelerating pace and scale of globalization driven by technological revolutions in communications and transportation and lowered trade barriers. These new developments began to transform globalization from a gradual process (one of many factors affecting economies and individuals) into a predominant factor molding our common reality. Japan conquered American markets, not American soldiers, which led to a fundamental reassessment of what was meant by the concept of national security.

What emerged in the 1980s as a direct result was a consensus of national security and foreign policy interests that extended beyond an exclusive focus on conflicts and added a major focus on economics. This new focus, in turn, was reflected politically when James Baker, a financier and then secretary of the treasury, became secretary of state. At this point, the people gathered around the table at foreign policy discussions changed. They were no longer solely generals and diplomats. Now economists and business leaders were taking leading roles. It was a highly effective transformation for U.S. foreign policy. Reflecting this new paradigm was the defeat of the Soviet Union, not by the Cold War, but because it was driven out of business.

The technological changes that spurred globalization in the 1970s and 80s accelerated even further in the 1990s. This change was so rapid over the past decade that the process of normal societal response and adjustment (a process that historically has required a time period spanning one to two generations) has been swamped. Even at this early stage of the Information Age, the global norm is instantaneous communication. The virtualization of financial markets has eliminated the need to move currency physically, and we have also seen an exploding capacity to move people and goods at relatively low cost and at nearly the speed of sound. "A chicken in every pot" has been replaced by "a satellite dish on every roof," or at least in every village around the globe. The Internet reaches virtually every country in the world. Clearly, this trend will increasingly take its place at the center of

Figure 1. Defining National Security Today

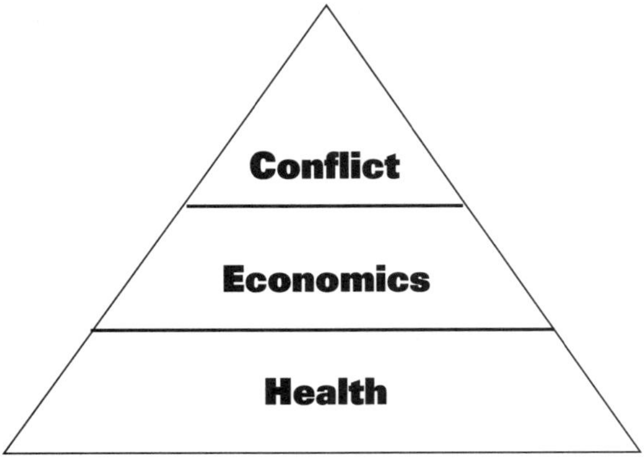

humankind's common reality in the 21st century.

Today, these trends are pushing the world toward yet another shift in the concept of what is meant by national security and, therefore, which interests are being served by foreign policy. I predict that within the next decade, health will be at the core of American foreign policy (Figure 1).

How can I distinguish this brash statement from that of the Hog Farmers Association? Let me start with perception.

GLOBAL HEALTH: THE HEART OF THE MATTER

In mid-May of 1999, the Global Health Council, in partnership with The Robert Wood Johnson Foundation and the Rockefeller Foundation, conducted a nationwide public opinion poll aimed at assessing what Americans know and think about global infectious diseases. In preparing for this poll, we conducted a series of focus groups around the country. One of the questions we asked concerned which issues people saw as national security issues. The first response we received (for the most part, it was what one would expect based on a world view still resonating with the conflicts of the Second World War and the Cold War) showed that national security was predominantly viewed as military security.

However, when we probed more deeply, respondents began describing their own view of personal security. At its heart, this concept of personal security revolved around the health and safety of their children, their families, and their communities. In that context, the people we interviewed perceived global health issues as very much at the center of their concerns for the future.

The poll itself, conducted in mid-May of 1999 among 1,201 randomly selected American voters, strongly reinforced this finding. It also revealed that 48 percent of all Americans knew someone who has suffered from one or more of the four global infectious diseases on which our survey was focused: TB, HIV, malaria, and hepatitis.[1] The problem of infectious diseases, as it turned out, is truly an issue that hits close to home in the United States. When asked to rate a set of global problems in order of importance, 70 percent rated the spread of global infectious diseases as very important. It is notable that, considering that we were currently in the midst of the war in Kosovo, this response was significantly greater than the 58 percent who rated regional and civil warfare as very important. We were struck by the centrality of this health issue in the perception of most Americans.

National security is not an abstract construct. In our democratic society, it is built on the individual security concerns of 280 million citizens. As noted, one of its two major functions is to protect vital national interests from threats from outside the country. There also is a strong objective basis to public concern with global health.

VERMONT: A CASE STUDY IN SECURITY

This evolution in the concept of national security is less surprising than it may seem. Let us consider a historical parallel. The early history of the state of Vermont, the fourteenth state to be admitted to the Union, was one of struggle against two powerful foreign colonizing forces—New York and New Hampshire—each claiming sovereignty over Vermont. Ethan Allen's Green Mountain Boys fought successfully against New York and New Hampshire for Vermont's freedom and, for a brief time, Vermont existed as an independent republic, ultimately deciding that joining the Union was in the state's best interests.

[1] Our list excluded some of the leading global killers, notably pneumonia and diarrhea, because these illnesses are so common as to have rendered our findings meaningless.

In those days, Vermont had a foreign policy directed at protecting the state from incursive neighbors. However, with the progressive integration of the states into the United States, this so-called foreign policy became irrelevant for Vermont. So, in many respects in this era of globalization, will it also become irrelevant for the United States.

However, issues concerning the spread of disease and the health and well-being of Vermonters continue to be at the heart of that small state's engagement with the outer world. Today, Vermont even has a physician as governor, and its Senators from both parties have been leaders on health issues both domestically and internationally. Vermont no longer needs a secretary of state, but it very much needs a commissioner of health. This same process is now under way globally.

But why should health, rather than some other issue, serve as the basis for our views of national security? Why should it sit at the base of the triangle? First, conditions of ill health around the world directly and indirectly threaten the lives of large numbers of U.S. residents. Second, the levels of ill health in those countries constituting a majority of the world's population pose a direct threat to their own national economic and political viability, which threatens our global economic and political interests as well. Let us not forget that fully 40 percent of the remarkable economic growth that the United States has enjoyed over the course of this decade has been driven by global trade in commerce. Our economic well-being is dependent on the rest of the world. Third, health-driven issues pose a very high risk for engendering or contributing to armed conflicts around the world that could directly affect our own military forces.

In fact, failure to address the major threats to global health could reverse the benefits of globalization. In a very real sense, microbes have responded more nimbly to the opportunities presented by globalization than we have. This dawning realization may explain why the World Health Organization (WHO) for the first time elected a Prime Minister of a country, Norway, to serve as its head.

U.S. NATIONAL INTERESTS

Whatever the reader's political views may be about President Clinton, we cannot help but appreciate his ability to identify a leading issue before it becomes conventional wisdom.

In 1992, his campaign staff insisted: "It's the economy, stupid," while George Bush stood on his demonstrated ability to deal with conflict. With the same kind of foresight (and for the first time in U.S. history) the Clinton Administration added a global health specialist to the staff of the National Security Council.

In a speech to the United Nations in 1992, President Clinton observed, "Only 2 percent of all global biomedical research is devoted to the major killers in the developing world. No country can break poverty's bonds if its people are disabled by disease and its government overwhelmed by the needs of the ill." This is certainly a clear challenge to the great centers of biomedical research represented by the Association of Academic Health Centers.

There are four key issues in global health that relate directly to U.S. national interests: infectious diseases, AIDS as a particular infectious threat, reproductive health, and the health and development of children around the world. Let us consider each of these issues in more detail.

ADRIFT IN THE MICROBIAL SEA

Over the past few years, it has become almost commonplace to hear that no microbe in the world is more than a day away from a U.S. port of entry. In his paper on the threat of bioterrorism (chapter 6), Dr. Hughes lays out the six factors that, according to the Institute of Medicine, underlie the emergence and reemergence of infectious diseases around the world. It is notable that four of these six factors involve economic and human dynamics outside the standard biomedical realm. Only the final two factors, microbial adaptation and the breakdown of health systems, are issues with which most academic health center leaders are comfortable.

Thanks to globalization, all of humankind today paddles in a single microbial sea. The developing world, in particular, is an ideal culture medium for the evolution, selection, transmission, and amplification of infectious microbes. Urbanization is proceeding at a breakneck pace in the poor countries of the world, and already today more than half of humanity lives in cities. Put five billion people into the tightly packed slums of the developing world, and we have the best foretaste of the world as it will look by the middle of the next century. Add to this concentrated formula a highly susceptible pool of people due to lowered host resistance as a result of chronic undernutrition and repeated infections. Marginal or nonexistent water and sanitation systems, exacerbated by a depletion of water resources, lead to ever-higher rates of enteric transmission, which complement the respiratory transmission encouraged by overcrowding. On top of that, the widespread use of suboptimal doses and courses of antimicrobials encourage the spread of antimicrobial resistance. Combine these established trends, and you have the nearly perfect generator of a wide array of infectious threats with a high potential for inflicting massive damage.

Had this happened in the 19th century, it might have occasioned limited concern on our part from a hard-hearted perspective; the victims of disease could die in situ without affecting us. However, today, two million people cross international borders every day: approximately one-tenth of humanity each year. Of these, more than one million people travel from developing to industrialized countries each week. This is an accelerating trend, and it cannot be altered without a seismic reversal of globalization and all that we have come to depend upon in terms of economic development.

Thus, global infectious diseases pose a true and growing threat to the United States. It is a bit surprising that so many people are coming to this realization so late, but perhaps that is human nature. It is noteworthy that already over the course of the last 50 years, at least five times as many Americans have died from communicable diseases that entered the United States from the developing world than died in all the military conflicts of the same period. West Nile encephalitis, which made the headlines, is only the most recent in what is likely to be a growing river of microbes that find their way from distant lands to our ports of entry. There has been an ironic, inversely proportional relationship of media attention to the number of cases of West Nile fever. In actual fact, far more urgent microbial threats exist in our country that receive little or no media coverage. They include the following:

1. *Antimicrobial resistance (AMR).* Anyone working in a health center today has seen an alarming increase in the rates of antimicrobial resistance

among both common and esoteric infections. However, many practitioners may not be aware of the degree to which antimicrobial resistance is being driven by the use and misuse of antimicrobials in developing countries around the world. I have worked in numerous developing countries, and I cannot think of one in which I could not walk up to a street vendor and very readily purchase any first generation antimicrobial, almost certainly any second generation, and very frequently a third generation. These are prescribed in small doses because they are expensive. Or they are taken only partially because those who need them try to economize by saving some medication for a later episode. Of course, this is the perfect selecting mechanism for microbial resistance.

When we look at the spread of resistant organisms in today's world, we can see it is a matter of weeks before a particular resistant strain identified by a laboratory in one part of the world pops up on another continent. This phenomenon has fundamental implications for health in the United States. We are a highly antibiotic-dependent health system. Many of our gains in combating communicable illness and reducing disease and mortality have been the result of the easy availability and wide use of antibiotics and antimicrobials.

If we face a 21st century in which this important arrow in our quiver is no longer as powerful as before, we will face profound ramifications. Over the past one and a half decades, the United States has already seen a significant increase in deaths due to infectious diseases.

2. *Tuberculosis (TB),* another underrecognized threat that, as you well know, was the great killer of the 19th century. When many of today's physicians attended medical school in the 1970s, TB was considered a disease of the past. Today, it has reemerged with a vengeance. It is estimated that nearly three million people around the world die each year as a result of tuberculosis. It is the second-leading cause of adult infectious death globally. Recently, we have seen the reintroduction of TB into the United States and the growth of multidrug-resistant TB. This is a profound threat to public health, and the cost of dealing with it is increasing significantly. It is notable that one-third of our registered TB cases in recent years have been among people who came to the United States from other countries.

What happens globally affects us domestically; it is essential that we realize this situation. What happens in this country is a direct result of what occurs around the world.

3. *Vector-borne diseases (VBD).* West Nile encephalitis is only the latest VBD to make the news in this country. However, malaria kills more than one million people a year around the world, primarily in Africa. The anopheles mosquito, the vector that transmits malaria, is endemic to the southern parts of the United States. In fact, the Centers for Disease Control and Prevention (CDC) was founded to combat malaria in this country. We may think that malaria is a disease of the past, but over the past several years, we have seen hundreds of cases of malaria in this country.

For the most part, these cases were imported, but a small number were transmitted within U.S. borders. With the advance of global warming and global climate change, the range of malaria vectors in the United States has expanded significantly up into the central Midwest and mid-Atlantic states. The mosquito's range today extends well beyond what it was in the days when malaria was a recognized public concern.

We clearly stand at risk for reintroduction of malaria, a situation that would have serious consequences in the United States. However, this is not the only risk we face.

4. *Dengue hemorrhagic fever.* An ongoing threat in parts of Asia, this disease is emerging as a major health threat in Central America and the Caribbean, and is certainly an issue within our own country. Residents of the southern regions of the United States need to recognize that this disease has considerable potential to affect them in the near future.

There is a wide array of infectious diseases that could pose a very real threat to the United States in the coming years. In addition, we face the threat of bioterrorism. This topic will not be addressed in this paper; it is a very specific national security threat, and it would be more appropriately considered in the context of a military-based approach to foreign policy.

HIV/AIDS: SCOURGE OF THE DEVELOPING WORLD

I have separated the issue of HIV/AIDS from the broader topic of infectious diseases because I believe that its threat to American national security is of a different nature. Although this disease has claimed hundreds of thousands of American victims, it appears unlikely to accelerate further in this country. For the time being at least, Americans have found the means to mute the consequences of HIV/AIDS through antiviral treatment. Nonetheless, U.S. foreign policy leaders should continue to be concerned about its direct and predictable effects in countries of the developing world. Fortunately, with the President's recent announcement of a $100 million AIDS initiative for Africa, this problem finally appears to be receiving some of the attention it warrants.

What are the dynamics of the AIDS pandemic outside the United States, and why is it relevant to our country? This year, over six million people will be infected with the AIDS virus. This will bring the total number of people living with HIV close to 40 million around the world. Current trends indicate that, by the year 2007, 100 million people will have been infected with HIV around the world. This is not just a series of individual tragedies; it is a massive tragedy for humankind, particularly for those living in less developed countries. Patients in the United States have benefited from the development of the so-called triple therapy, which has reversed the mortality trends of AIDS.

Unfortunately, triple therapy in the developing world is an empty solution. A therapy costing between $US10,000 and $US30,000 per person per year is simply an unrealistic option in countries that typically devote between $5 and $10 per year to health care per capita. Even with massive reductions in the prices of these drugs (a matter now being debated), the issue of followup is critical: To prevent the development of drug-resistant strains of HIV, it is crucial that patients receive and take the appropriate drugs regularly and maintain their therapies. Most developing country health systems are not, at this point, prepared to address these kinds of issues.

What will happen to the tens of millions of HIV-infected people in the developing world? Bluntly put, they will die. The sad bottom line is that those already infected are going to die, almost regardless of any solution we can imagine. They will die as adults in the prime of life, leaving their societies in disarray. We are seeing this in Africa right now. In Zimbabwe, the average life expectancy dropped from 62 to 37 a few years ago, purely as a result of HIV. We also are witnessing an enormous spread of HIV in South

Africa. In the Kwazulu-Natal province, fully one-third of all adults of reproductive age are infected with HIV. Additionally, 80 percent of the children in the local pediatric ward are HIV babies. HIV/AIDS will profoundly affect these societies as they lose more and more of their adult population. Very often in these countries, the people who are at highest risk of HIV infection are those who have made the leap into the middle class. As they die, and as their countries lose more and more community leaders, the resulting social disarray is virtually inevitable.

In addition, conservative projections place the number of AIDS-related orphans in Africa at 40 million by the year 2015, that is, 40 million young people without parents. The reality of the developing world today is that young people without parents, living in communities in which their extended families are equally smitten by the virus, have no place to go but to the streets of the growing cities of Africa.

The problem of street children in Africa is heartbreaking, but the more hard-nosed members of our society may be inclined to say that these children are not a national security concern for the United States. However, when we examine the history of conflicts in Africa over the past one to two decades, we find a very disturbing pattern: These children are being used as vehicles for armed conflict. One West African rebel leader has said that a 12-year-old is the perfect recruit because he is old enough to carry an AK-47 and old enough to understand and follow orders, but still too young to have compunctions about engaging in acts of terrorism and human degradation.

It is a terrifying prospect. When we consider the history of our nation's foreign military engagements over the past 50 years, we discover that only a few engagements (Vietnam and Korea) were classic, geopolitical engagements. Instead, there is an increasing trend toward U.S. military involvement in humanitarian situations. We saw it recently in Kosovo, and we saw it in Somalia. Given that Americans are unwilling to sit by and tolerate genocide and mass murder, it is very likely that the U.S. military will become involved in one or more of the growing conflicts in Africa. There are bound to be profound ramifications for the American psyche when network news shows depict adult GIs facing down 12-year-old African boys across a front line. Such images may affect the American public much the way the Vietnam War did. AIDS is a serious national security issue to our nation for that reason alone.

REPRODUCTIVE HEALTH

Global reproductive health is not a prominent image on the national security radar screen, but it should be. In this country, we recognize that a key element of good reproductive health is a woman's ability to choose the timing and number of her pregnancies. Far too often, this is not the case in the developing world.

The availability and use of voluntary methods of family planning, both reversible and nonreversible, have expanded enormously over the past quarter century, and the United States has played a leadership role in this global trend. However, the reality remains that there are more than 150 million couples around the world today who would like to limit or space their childbearing but lack access to effective family planning services and methods.

Congress has been debating the issue of U.S. foreign assistance for family planning for the past 5 years. The Conservative Right has used the domestic debate over abortion to restrict U.S. family planning programs abroad. As a result, budgets for these programs have been cut by one-third. Ironically, family planning programs are being reduced to a trickle just as the world population is burgeoning and the demand for these services is increasing. This phenomenon is doubly ironic: historically, U.S. foreign assistance has never been used to support or encourage abortion services, which is what the debate theoretically concerns. The abortion issue may well be something of a Trojan horse for those who are opposed to the fundamental principle of a woman's right to control her own fertility.

In the past 13 years, the population of humans on this planet has grown by one billion people, that is, our world has increased by the same number of humans alive on earth, in toto, when Thomas Jefferson was president. On October 12, 1999, the global total surpassed six billion people, twice the number of humans on the face of the earth when John Kennedy was elected president in 1960.

These statistics are not being examined from a demographic or population perspective. Six billion healthy and productive humans would not constitute a threat to U.S. security interests; quite the contrary. However, as noted earlier, a high proportion live in grinding poverty and suffer severe malnutrition. They are the unwitting stepping stones for communicable diseases. Desperate for better opportunities, they carry infectious diseases around the globe as they migrate to the developed world at a rate never before imaginable. This problem warrants our attention.

HEALTHY CHILDREN, HEALTHY WORLD

Child health and development constitute yet another compelling global health concern. Child health is often characterized as a humanitarian issue; indeed, it is in keeping with the basic values of a democracy. However, it is also profoundly important for the future of this nation and the planet. Eighty percent of the children born in this decade were born and are being raised in developing countries. Today, one-third of all adults in developing countries have some degree of cognitive delay or dysfunction as a result of childhood malnutrition or disease. It is an enormous loss of human potential. In a globalized world, these cognitively impaired adults will be our trading partners, our customers, our labor force, and our neighbors. This issue should be of immediate concern to the United States as we think about the future.

PLACING GLOBAL HEALTH FRONT AND CENTER

The fact is that global health belongs squarely on the map of national security and foreign policy. Its significance is driven, not by global health advocates, but by the practical realities of today's world. Yet, how global health is placed upon this map is vitally important. This is where U.S. academic health centers have a decisive role to play. Historically, this nation's institutions of higher learning have played a key role in the evolution of U.S. foreign policy. Geostrategists such as Henry Kissinger and Zbigniew Brzezinski were highly educated academics who also were well-versed in the interplay of military power. They were followed by a series of global economists, represented today by Secretary of the Treasury and former World Bank Chief Economist Larry Summers.

In the 21st century, foreign policy discussions will be driven by the leaders of academic medicine because they have the knowledge about health threats, health opportunities, and health realities. Academic medical professionals understand the health-related interplay between the United States and the developing world. In fact, this country already has models for effective interaction between U.S. health professionals and their counterparts around the world.

When considering world health, one may recite a litany of global health threats. Nonetheless, in no way does the future present a gloomy scenario. The new millennium offers the opportunity to make global health a reality. Each of the threats enumerated in this paper can be addressed constructively and rapidly to the benefit of all humankind.

History has already indicated that this is possible. According to a World Bank report on global health published in 1993, life expectancy as a function of per capita national income has improved steadily throughout this century.[2] In 1900, one could expect a life of 53 years. In 1930, at a comparable income, one could expect to live 60 years. In 1960, life expectancy was 65 years, and by 1990 it had reached 70 years.

What has changed the scene of life expectancy most dramatically is the advent of technology. Today, we have more means at our disposal for addressing the key issues of global health. This has direct implications for global health in the next century. As academics, researchers, and global health advocates, we need to focus more attention on the low-income end of the curve by developing technological strategies to improve health and longevity for the poor. President Clinton has pointed out that only 2 percent of all biomedical research focuses on the needs of the poor, who represent 80 percent of the burden of disease. Addressing this challenge falls within the realm of technology, and it is one major way in which the biomedical sciences can improve our common future.

How expensive is that future? Today, there are two billion people worldwide who are living on less than $2 per person per day. In its 1993 annual report, the World Bank examined what it would cost, given current levels of knowledge and programs, to provide a basic package of health services for the issues that this paper addresses: maternal and child health, reproductive health, infectious diseases, and prevention of HIV/AIDS. The

[2] World Bank. 1993. *World Bank Development Report: Investing in Health.* New York, NY: Oxford University Press

package cost, as established by WHO, is $15 per capita per year. The leaders of this nation's academic health centers can attest that the United States spends more than $4,000 annually on health care for every man, woman, and child in this country. Spending $15 dollars per person for two billion people means that the world could, to a significant degree, address the most compelling global health problems at a cost of $30 billion a year. It is not a major investment, particularly when viewed in the context of the investment our nation makes in military security.

HOW CAN ACADEMIC HEALTH CENTERS HELP?

U.S. academic health centers can contribute by investing in research and training. This will make a difference well beyond the current 2-percent level of investment that the President cited. Today, the National Institutes of Health (NIH) stands more ready than ever to address global health issues. Of all of the institutes comprising the NIH, the one institute whose budget has increased most rapidly is the John E. Fogarty International Center, NIH's institute for advanced study in the health sciences. This increase occurs at a time when NIH, as a whole, has prospered. It presents a great opportunity for academic health centers as well as an obligation.

Academic health centers in this country can also recognize their vital role and interest in health outside U.S. borders by offering programs in global health. Health educators in the United States are global leaders in health, and they should step up to the plate and make their presence felt around the world.

In the United States, what the public understands and wants (when conveyed via thoughtful and targeted advocacy on the part of respected leaders) can truly drive a policy agenda. We have made substantial progress in the global health arena in the Executive Branch of the Federal government, but this is not enough. The leaders of this country's academic health centers are in a unique position to influence Congress, as well.

As bills for international development assistance move through Congress in Washington's highly charged political atmosphere, the words of academic health center leaders—coming from a group that has not traditionally weighed in on foreign policy and foreign aid issues—could significantly influence those members of Congress who waver on this issue. It is a cheap vote to cut the budget for foreign aid. Academic health center leaders can encourage Congress to think otherwise. In addition, academic health centers need to support funding for the efforts of NIH, the CDC, and the Department of Health and Human Services as they address critical global health issues that pertain directly to this country. The CDC's Center for Infectious Diseases is conducting important work on these issues. In addition, NIH's Fogarty International Center is developing a research agenda to fund new and appropriate technological advances to improve health globally.

Finally, as spokespersons for health everywhere, academic health center leaders should recognize and honor the central importance of the World Health Organization. This organization is the 21st century's Department of Health for the globalized world, and it must be strong and effective. WHO now has an outstanding leader, Dr. Gro Harlem Brundtland. Despite this significant change in WHO's executive leadership, the U.S. Congress withheld its legally obligated dues to the UN. For too long, we have effectively held WHO and the Pan American Health Organization hostage to a domestic and highly politicized debate about abortion. This was simply wrong, and academic health centers should have spoken out against it.

Academic health center leaders also should support the Global Health Council (GHC). The GHC takes advocacy very seriously. It plays an important role in influencing political discourse and policy decisions, and it does so by engaging the skills of those with substantive technical knowledge. Global health policy decisions should not be left to politicians and paid lobbyists. One of GHC's top priorities is a series of global health forums to be held in locations around the United States. A number of these locations were selected strategically to target the Congressional representative representing the district where a forum takes place.

The GHC conducts these forums in partnership with local institutions, ideally with academic health centers, medical schools, and schools of public health. These institutions can attract participants and arouse public interest because they are well-respected in their communities and are known to speak out for the health needs of the local residents. It is the GHC's hope that health educators throughout the United States will help cosponsor Local-Global Health Forums, which draw people together on such topics as

AIDS in the community and in Africa, or the issue of reproductive health in the United States and abroad. Through these forums, GHC hopes to broaden the horizons of both the U.S. public and their political leaders.

CONCLUSION

Foreign policy exists for two clearly delineated purposes, and two purposes only: to protect vital national interests and to project core national values. The hard-nosed approach examines global health exclusively from the standpoint of national security interests. However, this country's finest moments occur when our policies and priorities are driven by our national values. We are a nation founded on the belief that all people are created equal and endowed by their creator with certain inalienable rights, among them life, liberty, and the pursuit of happiness. Life, liberty, and the pursuit of happiness are not conceivable in a world in which disease holds the upper hand. In today's world, no nation is an island. We are all in this together.

When it comes to global health, there is no them—only us.

2. *Health for All: Pipe Dream or Possibility?*

DAVID SATCHER

AS U.S. SURGEON GENERAL AND ASSISTANT SECRETARY for Health, I can attest that one of our nation's top priorities is taking a more global approach to public health. Today, for example, we are making a global commitment to optimal health for all based upon the Declaration of the Alma-Ata Conference of 1978.

However, before we consider health at the global level, we must examine our domestic health agenda. Over the past century, the United States has made tremendous progress. At the turn of the 20th century, a baby born in this country could expect to live approximately 47 years or, to be precise, 49 years if the baby was white, but only 33 years if the baby was African American. Today, U.S. life expectancy is approaching 77 for whites and 72 for African Americans. Clearly, we have made significant progress.

WHERE WE ARE; WHERE WE ARE GOING

The most dramatic progress has been in dealing with infectious diseases, which we have combated with a combination of improved sanitation and hygiene measures and vaccines and antibiotics. During the twentieth century, we eradicated smallpox and, by 1991, had also eliminated polio throughout the Western Hemisphere. Today, we are close to eradicating polio worldwide as long as we stay the course with the current and very powerful global public—private partnership in which Rotary International has played a significant role.

We also have made strides against lead poisoning by substantially reducing the levels of lead in gasoline in the late 1970s. Since 1950, deaths from cardiovascular diseases have declined by more than 60 percent, a decline that has continued throughout the 1990s albeit at a slower rate. Even with regard to injuries, we have made dramatic progress in the last 30 years, especially in regard to deaths from motor vehicle crashes. On a less somber but still important note, we have dramatically reduced the amount of dental caries among children thanks to the introduction of fluoridated water.

The 20th century indeed has been a great period in the field of public health, culminating in the decade of the 1990s. In 1990, when Dr. Louis W. Sullivan was Secretary of Health and Human Services, the United States announced its Healthy People 2000 program. It has met with both successes and failures, but as we head into another century, we can note that we have already accomplished at least 60 percent of the Healthy People objectives and accomplished virtually another 15 to 20 percent. In addition to the decline in cardiovascular deaths and injuries, the last decade has seen a decline in teenage pregnancy, homicides, and mortality from cancer, particularly breast cancer.

Unfortunately, we lack adequate data to evaluate the status of approximately 20 percent of the objectives. For another small subset, we either have made no progress or actually are moving in the wrong direction. Asthma is an example of this sort of backsliding: Since 1980, asthma has tripled among children under 5 years old, and asthma rates continued to increase throughout the 1990s among minority and inner-city children. Although we do not yet understand why we are losing this battle, we are making aggressive efforts to increase asthma-related research, education, and access to care.

Obesity also has increased dramatically during the past decade among both adults and children, but particularly among children. When we consider the rate of increase in recent years, we can see that childhood obesity is at nearly epidemic proportions in this country. It is a serious concern because obesity threatens to reverse much of the progress we have made in regard to cardiovascular diseases.

Furthermore, although smoking among adults has declined from 30 percent to approximately 23 percent since 1990, smoking among teenagers has increased significantly. Every day, more than 3,000 new teenagers become smokers despite all that we know about the dangers of smoking. The first surgeon general's report about the health hazards of smoking was published in 1964. Since then, 28 of the 50 surgeon general's reports have condemned smoking (including the report I released in April 1999 examining the problem of smoking among minorities). Despite all this publicity, smoking remains a major public health challenge.

Diabetes, too, has increased significantly in the 1990s, a trend that we believe is related to the increase in obesity, at least in regard to Type II diabetes. We suspect that it is related to an increasing lack of physical activity, especially among young people, and also to a significant rise in the amount of sugar in the average American diet.

These are the public health issues about which we are most concerned as we come to the end of Healthy People 2000 and prepare to embark upon the Healthy People 2010 program.

DOMESTIC HEALTH GOALS FOR THE FUTURE

In preparing for the next Healthy People initiative, we have decided upon two major goals. First, in examining the fact that life expectancy continues to increase in this country, we decided that, in addition to focusing upon the span of life, we need to put greater emphasis upon the quality of life. This is our first priority. Between the years 2000 and 2010, we will focus on quality-of-life issues, including the control of arthritis, osteoporosis, low-back pain, disabilities, and various secondary health conditions.

Our second, equally important goal is to eliminate disparities in health. As we leave the 20th century, we must face the reality that, despite tremendous strides in health care, we also have ended up with serious health disparities, particularly between different racial and ethnic groups in this country. It is a problem that we are determined to resolve. Making a commitment to "health for all" has no meaning if we do not commit to eliminating disparities in health. By this I mean a serious commitment behind which we are willing to put both our resources and our energy.

In 1980, the Surgeon General launched the "Healthy People 1990" initiative, which focused on reducing premature deaths among infants, children, adolescents, and adults. This continues to be a major component of our effort, and it is an area in which we have made real progress. We are determined to promote the ideal of preserving independence for older adults. In 1990, when we announced "Healthy People 2000," the focus was on increasing the span of healthy life, reducing health disparities, and increasing access to clinical preventive services. There also were several age-specific targets, which will continue in the Healthy People 2010 program.

How did we manage to narrow down all those diverse priorities to just two major goals? We shifted our focus toward increasing not only the quantity but also the quality of life. By doing so, we incorporated all the other goals. We also have taken significant strides toward making a commitment to eliminating health disparities. Many people are cynical about our ability to reach these dual goals, but they are realistic goals, and they can be reached if we are willing to make realistic efforts.

For example, we will need to focus on improving communication about public health. Half of the morbidity and mortality in this country is directly related to unhealthy behaviors such as smoking, physical inactivity, and poor nutrition. Health communication thus becomes a high priority, not to mention a major challenge. We must communicate the kind of messages that will have a real impact upon people's lives in both their homes and their workplaces.

We also need to strengthen the public health infrastructure, which is an area of serious need. In 1988, the Institute of Medicine reported on the flaws in the U.S. public health infrastructure, and these problems continue to this day. This is of particular concern in relation to the possible outbreak of infectious diseases. The state public health laboratories are not adequate to meet the challenge of an infectious disease outbreak despite dramatic progress during the last 5 years.

When our department decided upon this initiative, we began with those areas over which we had influence, especially those with significant disparities. We wanted to cover the needs of many minorities with the goal of making significant progress within 5 years. In this way, we could make any necessary adjustments, establish valid baseline measures, and link our current program to the Healthy People 2000 goals. We, therefore, decided to focus on six key health issues: cardiovascular disease, cancer, diabetes, HIV/AIDS, and child and adult immunizations.

TODAY'S GLOBAL CHALLENGES: COMMUNICABLE DISEASES

Which major global health challenges and opportunities do we face today and in the near future? First and foremost, we must finish the job of eradicating polio. With a highly effective public-private partnership in place to wipe out this disease, we are very close to eliminating polio worldwide. Ironically, now that we are so close to our goal, it is becoming more and more difficult to convince Congress to sustain financial support for this program. We are 98 to 99 percent there; we absolutely must not stop now. On a practical level, it just makes good fiscal sense: As we have explained repeatedly to Congress, once we no longer have to immunize against polio, we will save $250 million a year in this country and at least $1.5 billion worldwide. However, the most important gain in eradicating polio is the alleviation of human pain and suffering, upon which we cannot put a price tag.

The second global health challenge is the emergence (and reemergence) of infectious diseases. Without question, we live in a global community. Infectious diseases cross borders every day and do not need visas or passports to do so. Sometimes they come walking across the border, sometimes they come in cars, and sometimes they come on airplanes (even in first-class). Every day, infectious diseases cross borders. Two million people cross national borders every day around the world. Within 24 to 36 hours, a person can arrive anywhere in the world from anywhere else in the world. It should come as no surprise that infectious diseases are crossing borders.

On this and other health topics, we have to think globally. In a recent New York Times article, Larry Altman observed that, when those of us in medical training hear hoof beats, we do not think of zebras.* Whether or

* Altman, L.K. 1999. Encephalitis teaches an old lesson. *The New York Times,* September 28.

not you think of zebras when you hear hoof beats may have once depended on whether you live in New York or Africa. Today people travel all over the world. So we must think globally.

Only recently, New York City experienced outbreaks of an unusual form of encephalitis. When doctors sent samples of the disease to the Centers for Disease Control and Prevention (CDC), the center found the organism to be consistent with St. Louis encephalitis. (Even this type of encephalitis is almost a zebra, considering its rarity.) However, as it turned out, New York was actually dealing with West Nile encephalitis—a type of encephalitis that originated in Uganda in 1937.

In 1995, I chaired the Committee on International Science, Education, and Technology. We submitted a report to the President recommending that the United States work with international partners to develop a global system of surveillance and response to infectious diseases as a means of responding to emerging diseases. President Clinton signed that directive. Unfortunately, our progress in this initiative has moved slowly, primarily because we need competent laboratories strategically located throughout the world. We have been working with our G-8 partners on this project, but we still have a long way to go before we can rapidly detect and contain infectious diseases, especially those that have only recently been identified.

At the World Health Assembly in May 1999, Director-General of the World Health Organization (WHO) Dr. Gro Brundtland announced that one of WHO's major priorities will be the elimination of malaria. This priority is remarkable, given that malaria occurs primarily in very poor and developing countries. Approximately one billion people worldwide are exposed to the disease, and an estimated one million people die from it every year. Dr. Brundtland's decision made it clear that, unless WHO makes a commitment to rolling back malaria, it would not be acting globally as a global organization. She challenged all WHO member nations to commit to wiping out malaria. I am happy to report that in the United States, agencies such as the CDC and the National Institutes of Health (NIH) are making major contributions to fighting malaria by funding research, implementing programs, and developing new antimalarial drugs and vaccines along with drugs for other infectious diseases such as tuberculosis and other illnesses.

Another ongoing challenge we face on a global level is drug resistance. Resistance to penicillin by the pneumococcal organism emerged approximately 25 years ago in Southeast; it took almost 20 years for penicillin resistance to become a major issue in this country. The incidence of penicillin-related s. pneumoniae strains has been gradually increasing in the United States. Numerous other drug-resistant organisms have emerged. Drug resistance is a global challenge because once it emerges it spreads readily from one place to another. In Mexico, for instance, one can buy over-the-counter antituberculin drugs. This poses a threat to the health of people everywhere because it may lead to an increased incidence of drug-resistant tuberculosis all over the world.

Yet another global health concern is food safety. The food supply in the United States is without question a global food supply. The United States obtains 60 percent of its seafood from outside the country, as well as 40 percent of its fruits and 8 percent of its vegetables. We also send a significant amount of food to other countries. Maintaining a safe food supply is a global challenge. The reader may recall the recent outbreak of hepatitis that was traced to contaminated strawberries imported from Mexico. We also had a problem not long ago with raspberries from Guatemala that were contaminated with cyclospora. Very clearly to ensure the safety of our food supply, we must have a global strategy.

The same principle holds true as we strive to maintain the safety of our blood supply. It is truly unfortunate that we did not recognize hepatitis C until 1988 and lacked a test for screening it out until June 1992. An estimated four million people in this country are infected with hepatitis C, of whom approximately 7 to 8 percent contracted the disease from transfusions of contaminated blood. Similarly, in the early 1980s, half of all the hemophiliacs in the United States were infected with HIV from the blood supply. We still do not know where HIV started, but our experience clearly underscores the fact that the earlier we recognize a new infectious disease, the more effectively we can safeguard the health of people in this country and around the world.

TODAY'S CHALLENGES: NONCOMMUNICABLE DISEASES

Our problems are by no means limited to communicable diseases. We also are challenged globally by noncommunicable diseases. In 1998, noncommunicable diseases (primarily chronic diseases) accounted for 55 percent of all deaths worldwide. By the years 2010 to 2015, that figure could be as high at 70 percent. One of the major concerns is tobacco use. The World Health Organization has made a major commitment to promoting a new tobacco-free initiative. This program is similar to one that our department helped develop here in the United States. WHO's initiative includes a worldwide ban on smoking advertisements, an increase in cigarette taxes, and the implementation of smoking cessation programs. For the first time in its 50 years, WHO is exercising its mandate for a framework convention on the topic of tobacco control.

One remarkable irony of this new initiative is that, even though WHO has made this groundbreaking commitment to fostering a tobacco-free world, WHO's annual meetings are not themselves smoke-free. We introduced a resolution this past year to ban smoking at the World Health Assembly, but it was tabled until next year. Nonetheless, we will persist. We are determined to reach the goal of a tobacco-free world—beginning with the World Health Assembly itself.

Other noncommunicable health threats include violence and injuries. Recently, we have been working with colleagues in South Africa on this topic. South Africa's democratic structure has emerged beautifully in many ways, but its people have also experienced an increase in violence. We are taking a public health approach to this problem. In 1999, Attorney General Janet Reno and I met with colleagues in South Africa to discuss how the United States has tried to develop a public health approach to violence prevention. In addition, I headed up public health teams in Kenya and Tanzania following the bombing of our embassies there. It is a very powerful experience to witness the severe impact that such violence has upon a country and its people. We also learned during our time there that Kenya does not have an adequate emergency response mechanism for dealing with violence when it occurs. Now, a year after the bombing, we are still working with officials in Kenya and Tanzania, sharing our expertise in developing emergency response systems that someday may save as many lives every week as were killed in the bombings.

When we work together, even in response to crises, we move forward together. In Vietnam, for instance, injuries are a major cause of death. Today, under the leadership of Ambassador Peterson, we are working to implement an injury prevention system throughout the nation.

THE U.S. ROLE IN WORLD HEALTH

I am proud to say that the United States has been committed to global cooperation from the beginning. In 1924, at the first meeting of the Pan American Health Organization, U.S. Surgeon General Hugh Cummings was elected president. He proclaimed this nation's commitment to cooperation in the Americas. In 1948, when the World Health Organization was established, it was the U.S. Surgeon General who said that the world cannot exist half healthy and half sick. At the Alma-Ata Conference in 1978, the U.S. team made a leading commitment to the concept of "Health for All." Shortly after, the United States announced its Healthy People strategy. In 1998, when Dr. Brundtland reaffirmed WHO's commitment to Health for All, I was there along with Secretary of Health and Human Services Donna Shalala and Jo Ivey Boufford who represented us on WHO's Executive Committee.

The United States has been involved in making all of these commitments. We now have a responsibility to see them through. What will it take to accomplish this? It will take a global commitment, and it will take the kind of open, international discussion that the Association of Academic Health Centers supports and fosters.

It also will take a global communication network. We must have a global network in place that will enable us to communicate rapidly with our partners around the world on any issue. We also need a global system of surveillance and response that can rapidly detect and respond to any health threat anywhere in the world. This is especially important in regard to infectious diseases, but we also must collaborate globally to deal with other health threats, such as tobacco use. We need a global partnership for public health.

If we want to have Health for All, we need to support our bilateral agreements and our G-8 partnerships. We even need a global laboratory network. Along with colleagues around the world, we need to invest our energy, time, and funds in a global network.

We also need to support global organizations, such as the United Nations and WHO. It was painful for me to make the report from the United States to the Budget Committee this year because at that point the United States was still $35 million in arrears in WHO dues.

The commitment to global health, however, goes beyond paying the proper respect and monetary dues to these organizations. Health equity begins at home. We need to eliminate health disparities within our own country. This means developing a balanced community health system, making a commitment that every child will have a healthy start in life. It means proactively promoting healthy lifestyles and dealing with mental health from the standpoint of care and support and not of blame and stigmatization. It means establishing a system that gives all people universal access to health care in this country.

What is the role of academic health centers in making these commitments? The United States has always looked to its academic health centers for pioneering leadership in the health care field. For instance, we have looked to our health educators to conduct research in the treatment of AIDS, and that is where the effective treatment AZT was developed. As we pursue development of an HIV/AIDS vaccine, academic health centers will continue to play a key role.

In regard to this and other health issues, academic health centers must set the research agenda, which increasingly must be a global agenda. Even if all we wanted to achieve was optimum health within the United States, the agenda still would have to be global in scope. We also must improve health care training, not just in our country but all over the world. We need to promote international training programs such as the CDC's Field Epidemiology training project. This program, which trains public health leaders throughout the world, has been implemented in 18 countries, including Egypt, Zimbabwe, Uganda, and Mexico.

HEALTH CARE IN THE GLOBAL VILLAGE

When I became director of the CDC in 1993, my first trip was to Morocco for an international HIV/AIDS conference for the continent of Africa. It was the eighth such conference. For the first time, the conference brought in teenagers from all over Africa. They did this because the AIDS epidemic was increasingly affecting the younger population, and because dangerous health habits that put people at risk of contracting the disease often have their roots in a person's behavior as a child or teenager.

The teenagers at this meeting were actively involved in the proceedings. They led the parade. They attended sessions. They asked questions. They came to press conferences and pretended to be reporters. They also discovered that the new director of the CDC was at this conference. When they saw me, they kept whispering: "He's black! He's black!" The young people were eager to meet me, so one day I went over to their tent. I spent 2 hours talking with these teenagers from all over Africa.

They asked tough questions: Dr. Satcher, when will we have a cure for AIDS? When will we have a vaccine? Is America concerned about AIDS all over the world, or just in America? What is your commitment? As I listened to these young people, the first thing I noticed was how much they reminded me of U.S. teenagers. So I asked: "Can you tell me why teenagers tend to engage increasingly in such high–risk behaviors?" I talked about sexual behavior. I talked about violence. I talked about smoking. They sat there stone-silent. Finally, a young man from Botswana said: "Dr. Satcher, have you heard it said that in Africa we believe that it takes a village to raise a child? Well, you tell me: As Africa has become more urbanized, more like the United States, where is our village? Where are the people who raise children, who care about children?"

I can hear teenagers in this country asking the same questions. Where is our village? Where is our community? Where are the people who used to care about children being safe at school and at home and in the community? Where are the people who used to take care of not just their own children, but other people's children as well? Where are the adults who used to start physical activity programs—children's soccer, softball, and basketball—but now do not seem to have the time? Where is our community?

I have to admit that I did not have an answer then, and I do not have it now. I have struggled with it. I discussed this predicament not long ago with William Foege of Emory University. He said to me: "The real answer is that it now takes a global community to raise a child. The children in Russia cannot be safe unless people in this country are committed to their safety. People in sub-Saharan Africa or Egypt or India or elsewhere—we all live in a global community. It takes a global community to raise a child, and together we must make that commitment. That should be our major motivation.

This, in the end, is is my answer to the question of why and how we should promote global health. We must care as a global community and work together as a global community. There are no other options.

3. Setting the Global Agenda For Health

Jo Ivey Boufford

HEALTH IS ON TODAY'S INTERNATIONAL AGENDA IN unprecedented ways, at both national and global levels. There are a number of reasons for this interest. Before we discuss them, however, it is important to understand some of the critical influences that affect the health status of populations. Some of these may fall outside the strict definition of health care. For instance, a recent Canadian study of key health determinants identified personal health care as only one of numerous important factors (FPTAC, 1996). Education, housing, economic development, and employment were also shown to be important factors in maintaining health These findings confirmed earlier research indicating that a number of the variables affecting health are not subject to action by the personal health care system (McKeown, 1976).

Various researchers have examined these inconsistencies, including Canadian economists Lalonde (1998) and Evans et al. (1994) who developed the health field concept for policy work in Canada in 1987. In 1998, the U.S. Department of Health and Human Services considered the relationship between poverty and health in Health, United States (NCHS, 1998). Other factors currently under examination include working conditions, control over work environment, and social connectedness (Marmot et al., 1978; Argyle, 1996).

Indeed, research by McGinnis and Foege (1993) indicated that only 10 percent of all premature deaths in the United States were caused by a lack of access to medical care. The vast majority were attributable to high-risk behaviors such as smoking, alcoholism, obesity, lack of exercise, and substance abuse. Of these deaths, 20 percent were related to environmental factors and 20 percent could be traced to the individual's genetic makeup. In tackling such issues, the personal health-care system, including academic health centers, will require a focus that extends beyond the individual patient.

ARE WE SPENDING TOO MUCH ON PERSONAL HEALTH CARE?

In light of these statistics, it is remarkable to note that public health expenditures in the United States are heavily directed toward the personal health care system. This country currently spends more than 95 percent of the available health care dollars on about 10 percent of the avoidable early deaths (USPHS, 1993). This pattern is gradually changing, but the fact remains that in the United States, as in most other countries, health care policy making is dominated by the concerns of the personal health care delivery system. Within this system, decisions remain dominated by hospital-administered health care.

In recent years, greater attention has been focused on diseases that can be controlled or eliminated by preventive health programs such as those advocating for improved diet, tobacco cessation, and elimination of substance abuse (NCHS, 1998). This increased focus on preventive health care has raised the profile of global health policy, as is seen with such programs as the World Health Organization's (WHO) Health For All program and the Healthy People 2000 and Healthy People 2010 programs in the United States. Such initiatives have raised awareness about population health within the entire health sector.

Since numerous countries would be involved in developing an agenda for promoting global health, the topic has the potential to be quite broad.

Each country would focus on the health status of its own population, streamlining the program to fit its own unique culture and health care infrastructure. Each country also would need to shape its health policy to suit that nation's political will. Health agendas thus would vary dramatically from country to country.

Furthermore, to go forward with any global health initiative, each country involved would need to have proactive leaders. In addition to decisive leadership at the country level, strong leadership at the international level would also be needed.

Global leadership in this area has been fragmented over the past decade. Fortunately, that trend seems to be changing, thanks to the recent revolution in communications and transportation. We currently are seeing an unprecedented level of interest in global health based upon an increasingly common understanding that includes several virtually universal realizations:

- Diseases in one country can be readily transmitted to another through the movement of people, animals, food, blood, and low-quality pharmaceuticals across borders.
- Environmental degradation can have regional and often global consequences for air and water quality, land use, and food production.
- Chemical or biological weapons pose very real risks to every country.

DO HIGH-PROFILE DISEASES POSE THE GREATEST THREATS?

This "high visibility" global health agenda has focused primarily on infectious diseases (especially HIV/AIDS), bioterrorism, and the environment. These are the issues most frequently discussed by health officials and, increasingly, by the financial and political officials who have the power to set agendas and mobilize financial resources for global action.

The question is, Are these the real disease threats from a burden-of-disease perspective? The disability adjusted life years measure, or DALY, is used to express years of life lost to premature death and years lived with a disability, adjusted for its severity. One DALY is equivalent to one lost year of healthy life. If we look at the leading causes of the mortality and disease burden in 1998, we find that infectious diseases rank high on the top ten list for both premature death and disability (NCHS, 1998). However, the high-profile global health agenda seems to be missing the significant levels of heart disease, stroke, chronic pulmonary disease, cancer, and mental illness. Furthermore, when projecting ahead 20 years, we see that the disease burden shifts significantly toward chronic disease, mental illness, accidents, and violence—none of which we currently are prepared for on a global level.

BELOW THE TIP OF THE ICEBERG

Below the tip of the global health iceberg are equally important influences on health awareness with the potential to support global health initiatives at various levels. One is the power of market forces. The second (quite closely linked) is the power of ideas: For several decades within the social sector, people have been thinking about international health in a new light and taken action accordingly. New ideas are gaining acceptance in individual countries, in large part because this is a time of considerable instability in health sectors worldwide. Traditional models of organization and financing are being shaken in more and more countries. For instance, people are challenging the traditional dominance of the hospital in personal health care delivery systems. They also are questioning the value of disease-specific, vertical international assistance programs.

The high cost of the personal health care delivery system is an issue in most countries, and this problem promises to worsen. The United States is by no means the only nation facing an aging population, a rising incidence of chronic disease, and the increasing use of high-tech medical equipment and high-priced pharmaceuticals.

International funding agencies such as the World Bank and the International Monetary Fund have implemented "market solutions," which in turn have led to "structural readjustment." This approach includes decreasing the cost of government, reducing the share of public spending, diversifying provisions among public and private sectors, and encouraging foreign investment. In countries where virtually all health and social services are publicly funded, structural readjustment has caused some tension regarding how much money should be earmarked for support in these sectors and how much should be invested elsewhere.

READJUSTING OUR FOCUS: HEALTH INITIATIVES AND REFORMS WORLDWIDE

International health initiatives are starting to shape the way countries make health decisions. Beginning with the 1970s, nations began to look beyond their traditional health care delivery systems and health service indicators. A growing awareness emerged, at least among public health professionals, that health is integral to human development. This awareness engendered efforts to improve, develop, and track markers for health and social development, which supplemented purely economic development indicators such as a growth in gross domestic product (GDP).

Commencing in the 1970s, a number of major UN General Assembly global conferences and actions addressed the economic rights and duties of states (1974), population (1974), women (1975), human settlements (1976), and water and desertification (1977). In 1978, the Alma-Ata Conference articulated a health strategy based on primary care that called for equitable access to personal health care services. This strategy placed an emphasis on disease prevention and basic public health services, including clean water, effective waste disposal, and safe food (Gunatilleke and Hammad, 1997) and involved communities and nonhealth sectors in the decision-making process. The past 20 years have proven to be a powerful organizing principle in health care reform internationally.

At each of the UN meetings, the media showed great interest in global health issues. Health advocates from WHO, as well as from a variety of governmental and nongovernmental agencies, added sections on health to many of the conference reports. UN agencies other than WHO (especially the Child Health and Survival division of the UN Children's Fund (UNICEF) and the UN Fund for Population Action (UNFPA) Program on Population and Reproductive Health) launched increased health initiatives. In 1981, the World Health Assembly and UN General Assembly adopted these initiatives in their Health for All by the Year 2000 strategy, a program based largely on primary care. Several principles grew out of these initiatives:

- Governments are responsible for the health of their people. In turn, the people have a duty, individually and collectively, to participate in promoting their own health.

- Governments and health professionals should disseminate health-related information explaining health risks, health-promoting behaviors, available medical interventions, etc. They also should provide an infrastructure for the administration of health services, including appropriate venues for discussing public health concerns such as clean water, waste disposal, and safe food handling. Providing adequate information and having an effective health care infrastructure will enable people to assume more responsibility for their own health.
- Countries need to invest more resources in the health sector and make sure that these resources are distributed equitably throughout the population.
- Nations should implement programs and policies designed to focus more research on major global health problems.
- Governments need to set standards for, and monitor, the quality of their health care services, including technology and drugs.

The World Bank's 1993 annual World Development Report was devoted to health. Using the DALY framework, it examined the cost burdens of various diseases and their implications for economic development (World Bank, 1993). This report marked the beginning of a significant shift in the World Bank's economic development strategy with World Bank investment in the social sector moving from approximately zero in 1980 to 11 percent of total World Bank expenditures in 1996.

HEALTHY PEOPLE, HEALTHY NATIONS

More countries are realizing that disease prevention is cost-effective and that implementing primary care principles saves money. For nearly 30 years, WHO's programs and policies have promoted health through primary care principles.

Finally, research is emerging regarding the multifaceted nature of health and illness. In particular, studies are revealing a great deal about the social determinants of health, such as education, social supports, economic development, equity. Research on these topics is enabling countries to pursue more innovative strategies for promoting health.

During the 1990s, the UN convened a series of international policy summits: the Conference on Environment in 1992, the Conference on Human Rights in 1993, the Cairo Summit on Population in 1994, the Beijing Conference on Women in 1995, and the Copenhagen Summit on Social Development in 1996. All of these conferences had health issues on their agendas, but with an important new dimension: Heads of state and finance ministers were involved, not just health and development professionals.

Each of these meetings led to an international agreement committing to action plans addressing problems in the identified areas and signed by most, if not all, UN member nations. Each meeting has held or will hold a 5-year follow-up conference, culminating in progress reports to the UN General Assembly. All the meetings to date have focused on health issues, even in those few cases when health was not on the original agenda. Naturally, progress in the health care arena varies from nation to nation, depending on each country's capabilities, resources, and will. Nonetheless, there is no question that what we are seeing is a global set of commitments to health and a scorecard for evaluating each country's success in meeting those commitments.

Several important elements of the global health agenda have emerged from these recent UN meetings and reports. First, health has been recognized as a vital factor in a nation's development process. Although this may seem obvious to those of us in the health professions, it is still news to many countries. Heretofore, many international financing bodies, ministers of finance, and political leaders have seen health care as a non-productive sector, at least from a purely economic perspective— that is, it is a sector consuming resources rather than producing them. However, recent research has shown that a nation's health may in fact be a precondition for sustainable development. Without good health, children cannot learn and adults cannot work. In the absence of health, a society's medical costs escalate. Markets cannot grow without healthy consumers. In addition, the health sector is often one of the largest employers in a nation, and its financial stability can have a serious impact on national GDP and social stability.

These summits also continued to emphasize the issue of equity as both an economic and a social principle.

Second, health and economic disparities among populations, both within countries and between countries, may have a greater impact than poverty levels upon a nation's health. As a result, international development efforts are promoting equity in access to health care, education, safe food, clean water, and shelter.

Third, the inequities faced by women in virtually every society make them disproportionately affected by poverty and violence, as well as discrimination in access to education, financing, employment, and professional advancement.

PARTNERS IN HEALTH PROMOTION

Nongovernmental organizations (NGOs) are major forces for advocacy in these areas. They promote citizen participation, provide services, and, as needed, partner with governments to foster a nation's health and development. Admittedly, there is some controversy over whether excessive dependence on NGOs may deflect citizens from making appropriate demands on their governments. Some people also question whether NGOs can be held accountable for services and whether their multiple delivery groups actually fragment available services. However, the concept of partnership (i.e., that governments need NGOs to be effective) has increasingly been recognized as a given when strategies are developed for promoting a nation's health.

Corporations are also donating goods and services, sponsoring specific programs, and engaging in discussions about issues that affect them (such as international pharmaceutical policy). The issue of multinational corporations and businesses as partners in health and development is complex. Many UN leaders, national health officials, and NGO leaders are deeply ambivalent about the ability of such entities to balance their own interests with the broader issues of society.

It is especially important that the developed or donor countries recognize that many of these health issues apply to themselves, as well. In the United States, for instance, the impact of infectious diseases like HIV/AIDS, drug-resistant tuberculosis (TB), and even the recently identified West Nile encephalitis, have brought health issues to the forefront of citizen concern—

and citizen concern is a critical factor in fostering political will and action.

In 1997, the G-8 Conference (the group of countries with the world's largest economies) placed health issues on its agenda, with a commitment to controlling infectious and parasitic diseases, promoting vaccine development, and cooperating with UNAIDS (the UN organization cosponsored by the World Bank and WHO dedicated to combating HIV/AIDS). This commitment was reaffirmed at subsequent conferences over the next 2 years, and the issue of food safety was added to the agenda. Finally, the Cologne Debt Initiative, initiated in 1999 at a meeting of G-7 finance ministers, laid out the framework for debt forgiveness by international and bilateral financial agents to reduce poverty and "assure that more resources are invested in health, including AIDS prevention, education, and other social needs essential for sustainable development" (Cologne Debt Initiative, 1999). Clearly, national political leaders and their finance ministers have issued a call for action.

Other issues "requiring concerted action by many nations" are being added to the list of global health concerns (Cologne Debt Initiative, 1999). The ever-visible infectious diseases, environmental hazards, and bioterrorism head this list. A number of other topics also offer potential opportunities for global cooperation (LeRoy, 1999), as follows:

- Population change attributable not only to family planning but also to aging, migration, and war.
- Food production and safety.
- Information and communication systems for the surveillance of health and disease.
- The development of infrastructures to respond to various health threats.
- Standard-setting for drugs, products, and devices.
- Occupational health and safety.
- Megascience research projects that are capital intensive and/or require multiple studies.

In a recent address to the UN General Assembly, President Clinton devoted almost half of his speech to the importance of poverty alleviation, education, and health in sustaining economic development. Also in the United States, a series of reports in the past 2 to 3 years, such as those published by the Institute of Medicine's Board on International Health (IOM, 1997) and by the New York Academy of Sciences (NYAS, 1996), have emphasized that it is in America's best interests to engage actively in promoting global health. These reports have stimulated new segments of the health community to look beyond our borders. The Council on Foreign Relations currently is conducting a study to assess the role of health in U.S. foreign policy and the best way to elevate its importance on the foreign policy agenda.

IN SEARCH OF THE BEST GLOBAL HEALTH LEADER

If an effective agenda for global health includes action at the multinational level and support for individual country action within agreed frameworks, where do we look for global health leadership? The most obvious candidate is the World Health Organization (WHO). Although international health cooperation precedes the establishment of the League of Nations, WHO was formally created in 1945 as the only organization in the UN system dedicated to health. With five regional offices, WHO is also the only organization currently positioned to provide a global perspective and act globally on broad population health issues.

WHO is governed by a 33-member executive board, with proportional representation from each region of the world. Its World Health Assembly is made up of 191 member nations, all in good financial standing. Its annual budget is about $US850 million. Slightly less than half of this money (the so-called regular budget) comes from fixed dues paid by member countries for general support. The other half (extra-budgetary funds) are allocated variably for specific projects by foundations, governmental donor agencies, and multilateral funding agencies. These projects have historically focused on a particular country, region, population group, or disease entity.

As with any large organization, WHO has gone through varying periods of effectiveness, and the past decade generally has been considered a low point. This has been particularly frustrating since it has come at a time of growing concern about international health issues and the growing need for mechanisms to facilitate cross-national action.

During the recent period of WHO's relative ineffectiveness, other UN agencies stepped into the gap. In particular, the United Nations Children's

Fund (UNICEF) has advocated for child health and survival, while the United Nations Population Fund (UNFPA) has worked on women's reproductive health and family planning. The World Bank has become a major funder of international health programs, and 3 years ago, UNAIDS was established as a multiagency program. There is some conjecture that UNAIDS was developed to make up for WHO's failure to create the kinds of multiagency relationships within and outside the UN that are needed to tackle the epidemic effectively.

THE FUTURE OF WHO: NEW LEADER, NEW DIRECTIONS

In 1998, in a highly contested election, Dr. Gro Harlem Bruntland, former prime minister of Norway, was elected director-general of WHO on a strong reform platform with wide-ranging support. She has moved quickly to create an organizational structure designed to break down the barriers between WHO's categorical programs. She also seeks to establish clear priorities for international health action against high-burden diseases in those countries that are in greatest need. Dr. Bruntland plans to strengthen the organization's normative functions to better enable WHO to lead in international standard-setting and strengthening the health systems of its member nations.

In addition to her proposed changes, Dr. Bruntland is promoting her agenda-setting efforts through a strong communications program, which is raising WHO's visibility among key political, financial, and health care decision makers. She is striving to develop effective working partnerships and is seeking extra budgetary resources or in-kind support from member countries, international lending agencies, private foundations, and the corporate world. Dr. Bruntland also has made a considerable investment in the new Evidence and Information for Policy Making program, whose goal is to set up a data-based system for setting health priorities, evaluating disease burdens, and implementing effective interventions.

It is still too early to determine whether the changes proposed by WHO's new leader will revitalize the organization and activate more effective health initiatives. Still, there is no question that WHO has been infused with a new sense of energy and credibility. The organization promises to once again become a powerful vehicle for improving global health,

Today, WHO's key missions, described below, are much the same as they were when the organization was founded, although the world is much more complex and the demands for health care delivery are much heavier (Boufford, 1995).

1. WHO should serve as the entry point (at the country, regional, or global level) to a worldwide network of health expertise.
   A. Its core staff should be senior, experienced public health generalists who can develop and manage the kinds of complex relationships needed to work with and through other organizations.
   B. Most of the organization's work should be conducted through partnerships with WHO Collaborating Centers, universities, labs, NGOs, and corporate entities. These partnerships should have explicitly defined cooperative agreements and outcome expectations for both long- and short-term projects.
2. It is critical that WHO sustain its normative function at a high level by convening world experts from the public and private sectors to:
   A. Set standards to raise the overall quality of health services, pharmaceuticals, equipment, health industries, public health practice, and workforce preparation.
   B. Devise guidelines for service-based, clinical and public health practice.
   C. Develop global health indicators to be used alongside economic indicators as part of a development report card on global health status.
3. WHO should maintain surveillance of global health status through information systems and tools for management and measurement. Such options should ensure that WHO can readily recognize major health threats. The organization should be able to predict health issues through a careful examination of demographic patterns, including migration due to war, environmental trends, and health patterns. In addition, WHO should assist countries in developing preventive interventions.
4. WHO should have the ability to mobilize limited specific or global action to:

A. Address threats (urgent response).
B. Prevent potential threats (via developing infrastructures for disseminating safe water, food, immunizations, etc.).
C. Develop diverse relationships appropriate to each country's or region's burden of illness and stage of development, with a special focus on the most vulnerable countries.

To be effective in these activities, WHO must serve as a role model by doing what we claim all health leaders should do. It should work intersectorally across traditional boundaries and mobilize communities for health. It should educate multiple publics about the determinants of health through effective use of the media, among other tools. WHO also needs to promote collaborative development of a global health agenda and help clarify the roles of the various sectors and stakeholders.

WHO's strategic documents assert that health must be put at the center of the worldwide development agenda. If we are to achieve ideal public health, health leaders around the world must work in partnership with leaders both inside and outside the health sector. Thus, the fact that there are many other UN and non-UN organizations active in health-related issues should be seen not as a threat but as an opportunity.

WHO's normative functions are unique and have the potential to make it the world standard-setting agency for health in areas such as pharmaceuticals, chemical safety, food quality, medical devices, biologics, and clinical services. If it accomplishes these goals and can work effectively with other international agencies, such as the World Trade Organization, the World Intellectual Property Organization, the Food and Agriculture Organization, and the International Labor Organization, WHO will have enormous potential for raising quality and consistency in critical health areas.

It is clear that, with sufficient funds or visibility, any organization, whether governmental or private, can effectively bring important issues to the world's attention. Recent examples include George Soros's interest in drug-resistant TB, the First Lady's involvement in mobilizing a special focus on AIDS in Africa, and Bill Gates's investments in maternal mortality, immunizations, and vaccine development. However, when the question arises as to which organization has the worldwide infrastructure and credibility to lead a global health campaign—or which organization has the credibility to convene experts on a global health problem—the answer is the World Health Organization.

ACADEMIC HEALTH CENTERS' ROLE IN WORLD HEALTH

Given these emerging frameworks for health and development and the necessary infrastructure for implementing effective action, what role can academic health centers play? There are numerous possibilities, but among the first would be to become more active advocates for global health. Although much of the work in the field of international health is conducted by health care experts (many of whom are faculty members in academic health centers), it has heretofore been uncommon for educational institutions to become directly involved in significant advocacy or action on the topic of global health. Many academic departments or units serve as WHO Collaborating Centers, but due to the historical vagaries for gaining and maintaining this status, this often has meant little more than an honorific title on the school's letterhead. Recently, WHO initiated efforts to make Collaborating Centers more active partners in international health actions. With these efforts under way, academic health centers now have an opportunity to lobby for high standards and clear contractual agreements with WHO. They also can press aggressively for better access to WHO's critical resources.

In addition, academic health centers can and should instigate more research into global health to raise awareness of, and garner support for, those health problems that create the greatest disease burden with a disproportionate impact on poor countries. Health educators and researchers have a critical role to play in this task, whether they function as individual institutions or work through international consortia. In 1999, the Rockefeller Foundation, the World Bank, and WHO joined forces in support of a Global Forum for Health Research, whose goal is to secure funding for a more coordinated research effort in regions of the world with a high burden of disease. This program will facilitate collaborative efforts while establishing an effective research infrastructure in developing countries.

Another area of great need is resource development in the fields of science and health. Unfortunately, WHO's capabilities in this area are minimal. This is where academic health centers have an opportunity to step in: Their educational institutions have the expertise in issues of workforce planning, training needs, and academic and clinical standard-setting.

It is critical for the United States to sustain and develop the burgeoning interest in global health currently being seen in Congress and among nongovernmental leaders. Academic health centers can play a pivotal role in advocacy by lobbying persuasively for more effective international health policy, programs, and investments.

LOOKING AND REACHING BEYOND OURSELVES

In today's economic environment academic health centers are justifiably preoccupied with advocating for their own institutional financial health and the sustainability of their clinical, research, and academic enterprises. However, it is possible for health educators to advocate for increased domestic funding and also lobby for more international health education programs. Academic leaders have enormous credibility in the community. They could give a powerful boost to health funding, especially funding for foreign assistance budgets, which currently are declining in all too many instances. For instance, the voice of academic health centers should have been heard in protest against this nation's failure to pay UN dues, a failure that adversely affected our credibility in a variety of international arenas.

Finally, it is very important for health educators to increase and expand the opportunities to students for learning about international health issues. They must go beyond short, elective experiences in clinical care or humanitarian relief. Students are the health care providers of tomorrow, and they need to see below the tip of the iceberg when it comes to global health. They need both first-hand experiences and academic instruction that helps them recognize such issues as the role of health in economic development; the importance of social equity in health; the role women play in a community's economic development; and the importance of partnerships within and outside the health sector to achieving population health. Today's students must appreciate that these issues apply in the United States as well as abroad;

when we participate in international service programs, we have as much to learn from other countries as we have to teach them.

REFERENCES

Argyle, M. 1996. The effects of relationships on well-being. In *Building a Relational Society: New Priorities for Public Policy*, N. Baker, ed. Hampshire, England.

Boufford, J. 1995. *Priorities for WHO's Role.* (Draft paper) Available from author.

Evans, R, Barer M, and Marmor T. 1994. *Why Are Some People Healthy and Others Not? The Determinants of Health of Populations.* New York: Aldine de Gruyter.

FPTAC (Federal, Provincial, and Territorial Advisory Committee on Population Health). 1996. *Report on the Health of Canadians.* Toronto, Ontario: Minister of Public Works and Government Services.

Global Forum for Health Research. 1999. *The 10/90 Report on Health Research.* Geneva, Switzerland: Global Forum for Health Research.

G7 Finance Ministers. 1999. The Cologne Initiative. *Report of G-7 Finance Ministers to the Cologne Economic Summit.* June 18.

Gunatilleke G. and Hammad A., eds. 1997. *Health: The Courage to Care.* Geneva, Switzerland: World Health Organization.

IOM (Institute of Medicine), Board on International Health. 1997. *America's Vital Interest in Global Health.* Washington, DC: National Academy Press.

Lalonde M. 1988. The Andrew Patullo Lecture: Health service managers or managers of health? *Journal of Health Administration Education,* 6(1):71–83.

LeRoy L. 1999. International grant making by U.S. foundations. *Journal of Health Affairs,* 18(3):234–238.

Marmot M, Rose G, Shipley M, and Hamilton P. 1978. Employment grade and coronary heart disease in British civil servants. *Journal of Epidemiology and Community Health,* 32: 244–49.

McGinnis J and Foege W. 1993. Actual causes of death in the United States. *Journal of The American Medical Association,* 270(18):2208.

McKeown T. 1976. *The Role of Medicine: Dream, Mirage, or Nemesis?* London: Nuffield Provincial Hospital Trust.

NCHS (National Center for Health Statistics). 1998. *Health, United States, with*

Socioeconomic Status and Health Chartbook. Hyattsville, MD: Centers for Disease Control and Prevention, Department of Health and Human Services.

NYAS (New York Academy of Sciences). 1996. *Global Cooperation in Science, Engineering, and Medicine.* New York, NY: NYAS.

U.S. Public Health Service. 1993. *The Core Function Project.* Washington, DC: U.S. Department of Health and Human Services.

World Bank. 1993. *World Bank Development Report: Investing in Health.* New York: Oxford University Press.

FROM AGENDA-SETTING TO ACTION

4. Learning About and Learning From Others' Experiences

THEODORE MARMOR AND JOHN PAKUTKA

THE SEARCH FOR NEW WAYS OF THINKING ABOUT health care policy and management today arises in part from the struggle of academic health centers to remain fiscally solvent while working continually to improve the quality of clinical care, research, and teaching. All these efforts must be made despite these difficult times of managed care and the Balanced Budget Amendment freeze. Indeed, much can be learned about global health care policy experience from the experiences of other countries. However, there also is great danger that nothing useful will be learned from the effort. We also should realize that translating the lessons into action does not necessarily require a change in national policy. An academic health center, on the other hand, can adopt internal policies that ensure that international cost control successes can be replicated.

However, using the proper approaches, we can apply the lessons learned from other systems to our own. The discussions during the early 1990s about health care could have benefited from less indulgence in the myth that the United States is unique. We would have been better served by opening ourselves to the idea that the United States has a great deal to learn from other countries. We should have been drawing on successful foreign and historical experiences, and setting about the serious work of revising and adapting suitable financing arrangements for today.

Nothing in the United States makes universal health insurance impossible to implement. However, propaganda, funneled through a largely uninformed media, has managed to spook the politicians. This occurred despite the polls indicating public support for the idea of universal health insurance. So it was that the great debate over national health insurance, which was revived by the Clinton Administration in 1993, died a quiet and disappointing death by the summer of 1994.

The fate of U.S. health reform under the Clinton Administration is not the subject of this paper, but the debate over universal insurance is an illustrative case in which cross-border learning, although needed and available, was both wildly unreliable and unhelpful in the distorted presentations traveling across borders.

LEARNING FROM OTHERS

Comparative policy studies such as these are subject to two fallacies, either of which may distort the subject. One, which may be labeled the World Cup fallacy, is the notion that cross-national learning is like picking the best soccer team: The task is to find the best model (technique, system, payment policy) from around the world, and then transplant it elsewhere. This approach is basically foolish. No institution, policy, or program is directly transferable in such a simplistic way. Nonetheless, we continue to see a market for one-size-fits-all reforms. They continue to be the topic of articles, speeches, and, most of all, conferences about the state of health care.

The other danger when conducting comparative policy studies is the opposite fallacy: The notion that, since nations always differ in some respects, we can never learn policy lessons from one another. This might be called the fallacy of comparative difference. It is a familiar weapon in the policy wars of any nation. Fortunately, between these two extremes lie other, more reasonable approaches. These methods for policy analysis, explained below, enable us to develop realistic uses for reasonable comparative analyses.

LEARNING FROM OTHERS: TRANSPLANTABLE GENERALIZATIONS

There are two possible bases from which we may draw strong policy lessons from the experiences of other countries. One is to consider what can be learned from similar nations. If conditions in another country are broadly comparable economically, politically, and/or culturally, one can be reasonably confident that a particular policy in that nation would be applicable within one's own society. That is, Country A's policy could be implemented in Country B with roughly the same results. Policy transplantability is closely linked to structural similarity. (To an outsider, the Nordic nations appear to provide many examples of this process.)

This method of learning from others, however, has certain limitations. The primary problem is that sometimes the most promising, appealing, or compelling answers to a particular policy question can be found elsewhere, in a very different sort of society. What, then, are we to do? Not a thing, necessarily, other than to be aware that this may be the case. In other words, we must strive to keep in mind that learning about another nation's experiences is not the same as learning from them.

There remains one other form of lesson-drawing that is rare, but powerful. Some describe it as generalizing from the widest variety of cases. It is the very opposite of a "similar system" design. That is, if a policy generalization holds true over many divergent cases, we may conclude that a powerful factor is at work—a factor that policy makers and administrators ignore at their own (and their constituents') peril. The logic behind this theory is straightforward: If Q follows from policy X in countries A to T, why should another nation (e.g., the United States) believe its experience will be different? This is the point of view behind the theory of transplantable generalizations. Just as the most similar design narrows the range of findings, so too does the most different design narrow the scope. However, in the latter instance, we are narrowing not countries but the likelihood of encountering a large number of such transplantable generalizations.

For example, let us consider the cost of implementing new policies that almost always turns out to be significantly higher than the policy advocates predict. Another example is the proposed wholesale transformation of the ways in which doctors are paid (a goal cherished by most health policy analysts) that, in fact, is almost never a practical option. Realizing and accepting this lesson regarding transplantable generalizations has important and very pragmatic implications for the debates about payment policy and its proposed reforms.

We begin by examining the most serious barriers to cross-national learning that, once they are removed, would substantially simplify the task of learning about and then from other cultures. After considering these barriers, we will learn about others by examining the set of existing data on health system performance in selected Organization for Economic Cooperation and Development (OECD) nations. We will study the data so we can understand the range of experiences among these nations. Third, while continuing to learn about different country experiences, we will analyze health system constructions and the cost-control mechanisms so we can understand the rich and varied character of their experiences. With this in mind, we will suggest what might be learned from international experience, and we will suggest one way in which this knowledge might be applied to an academic health center in the United States. Finally, we shall consider health reform as a global trend and examine the value of international conferences.

BARRIERS TO CROSS-NATIONAL LEARNING

A variety of myths can prevent one from learning important lessons from other countries' experiences in the financing and delivery of health care. The most important is a misconception that can be termed the myth of infantile yearning. All too often we search for a perfect world in the field of health policy. However, no system of health care financing is either free of problems or easily administered. We cannot avoid the gap between wishes and facts. The relevant inquiry is whether the problems associated with a particular health system are more serious than those linked to another.

For example, as the last industrial democracy without universal health insurance, the United States at least has the advantage of being potentially able to learn from nearly a century of experience with national health insurance elsewhere in the industrialized world. Canada's path to, and experience with, universal health insurance is a useful object of inquiry.

The United States shares with Canada a common language and political roots, a comparably diverse population with a similar distribution of living standards, and increasingly integrated economies. We also share a tradition of fractious but constitutionally based Federalism, a phenomenon that makes most North American political disputes similar (although not identical). Moreover, until Canada consolidated its national health insurance in 1971, North American patterns and styles of health care were nearly identical. (This similarity of care had been the case for so long that, until well after World War II, Canadian regulators used the U.S. Joint Commission on Hospital Accreditation to judge the credibility of their hospitals and medical schools.)

If public financing of health care has worked reasonably well in Canada, one might think it should work in the United States as well. This, at least, was the plausible premise of most of the favorable U.S. commentary about Canada's national health insurance program during the past health reform debate. Let us reiterate, however, that learning from the experience of others does not mean that one simply can import another country's institutional form of universal health insurance. The most enlightening comparisons seldom indicate that a foreign program, whatever its virtues, can simply be transplanted from one country to another with identical results. Nonetheless, the U.S. debate has been characterized not by cross-national learning but by myth-making, largely inferred from anecdotes told by critics of national health insurance about the Canadian experience.

The average person in the United States may not believe that dying Canadians are wading across the Niagara River to obtain access to life-saving health care; however, our public discourse is rife with overblown anecdotes about Canada's shortages, waiting periods, and long queues. What often is not reported in such accounts is the possibility that these drawbacks may serve as effective rationing mechanisms for elective and often unnecessary procedures, such as high-resolution imaging. Indeed, they may prove to serve as a more effective rationing mechanism than the U.S. micromanagement of doctor-patient relations.

Another myth may be called the left-pocket myth that misleads people into thinking that public health expenditures are more economically damaging than private health expenditures. Consider the significance of managing health care under public auspices and through public budgets: A few Canadians believe that all would be well if only there were private arrangements to augment the overburdened public system. However, the productivity and growth of the Canadian economy does not depend on how much health care financing flows through the public sector (the "left-hand pocket"). Nor does the growth of the American economy depend upon how much finance flows through the private sector (our "right-hand pocket"). The fact is that health care services represent current consumption. As such, they drain resources from investment, research, and productivity; they do so no matter whose budget they flow through or from which pocket they are drawn.

It is worth remembering that the OECD nations share a number of economic troubles. These nations have been rightly concerned about lagging productivity and, from a worldwide standpoint, modest levels of economic growth. Future economic competitiveness will depend upon investment in human as well as physical capital. Therefore, current consumption must be restrained if noninflationary investment is to have a future.

The current U.S. savings rate is anemic by any standard. The Canadian rate is not impressive either, except in comparison to that of the United States. The future economic health of any country will rely heavily upon its ability to cope with the pressure of increasing health care costs. To cope with the costs by painting mythical pictures of foreign experience is downright dangerous. To avoid that danger, we must take care to interpret the selective and sometimes seductive glances that are cast across national borders.

INTERNATIONAL HEALTH SYSTEM DESIGN AND PERFORMANCE

Any effort at comparative analysis must begin with the selection of the comparison set. To do this in health care, it is helpful to note the enormous disparity in health spending between developed and developing nations: Eighty-nine percent of worldwide health spending occurs in countries with 16 percent of the world's population (Scheiber and Maeda, 1999). To learn from comparative health policy analysis, U.S. observers first need to select those countries about which we hope to learn. The choice should be made from the variety of high-income nations in both the West and Far East.

By doing this, we in no way mean to trivialize the wide disparity of cultures and health care policies around the world. Ignoring the health problems of the developing world is arguably immoral and certainly foolish in a world in which a morning case of West Nile Fever can be transported to New York City on the afternoon flight. However, for the purpose of helping academic health centers learn relevant policy lessons from international experience, we must choose a comparator set of countries whose economic and social conditions are broadly similar to those in the United States. Based upon these criteria, we believe that Canada, the United Kingdom, Japan, and Germany are the ones most similar to the United States. The question then is: What do we know about their health systems in relation to the health system in the United States?

The United States stands alone among developed nations in its reluctance to guarantee health insurance for necessary health care services to all of its citizens (figure 1). (Germany makes its program optional.) This is not to say that uninsured Americans cannot gain access to the system. However, financial considerations do weigh heavily upon the 44 million uninsured U.S. residents, as well as upon their caregivers.

Figure 1. Health Insurance Coverage in Five Industrialized Nations, 1998

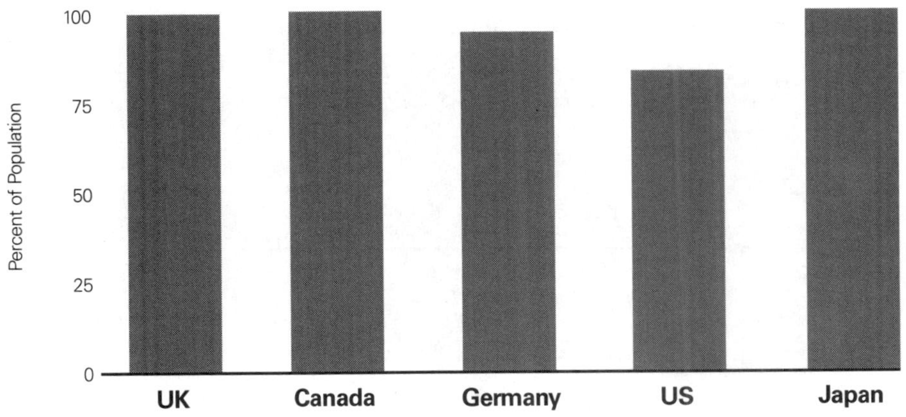

Source: OECD Health Data 1968.

The use of terms such as "socialized medicine" in political debates only clouds the real issues by creating more fear than understanding. Among the cited countries providing universal health insurance coverage, each has developed its own, distinctive system based upon a variety of factors, including sources of financing and sector of health care delivery, that is, public, private, or a blend of the two (figure 2). Many other dimensions also are involved, such as the type of private financing (personal premiums or employer mandates), type of public financing (national, state, or mixed), method of payment (fee for service, capitation, or salary), cost control method (global budget, capital expenditure controls, or provider competition), and degree of provider autonomy. By considering all of these elements, we can see that Japan, Germany, Canada, and the United Kingdom have developed coverage policies that meet their own, unique needs. There are many ways in which the United States could insure all citizens for necessary health care.

Spending in developed nations has been growing over the last four decades, consuming ever-larger shares of real income. In this regard, the United States stands out, spending 30 to 50 percent more than other nations (figure 3). If we were buying improved health with our augmented spending, this would make good sense. But do we?

Health outcomes can be difficult to measure, and even more difficult to interpret. Because outcomes are difficult to determine, we are left with

Figure 2. Financing Mechanisms in Four Industrialized Nations

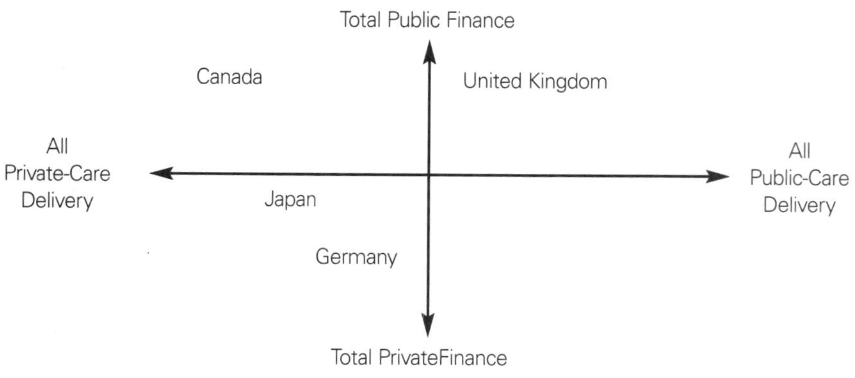

Figure 3. Health Spending in Five Industrialized Nations, 1960–1998

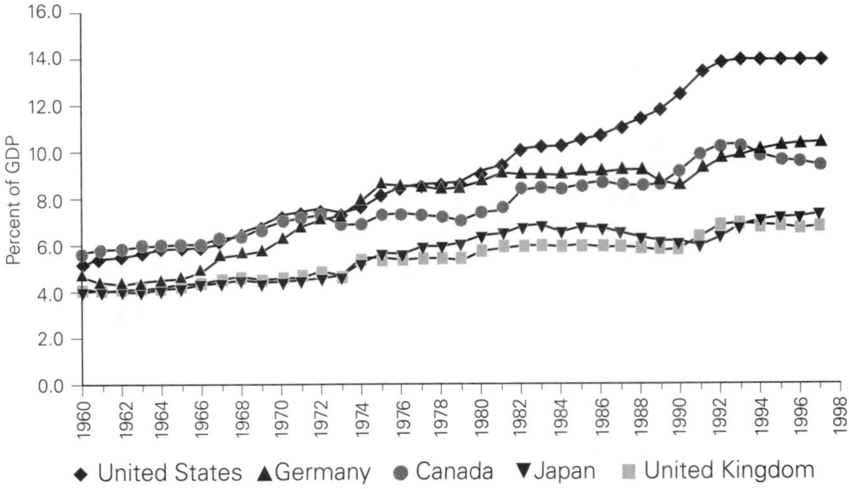

Source: OECD Health Data 1998.

the bluntest of measures, and because they are difficult to interpret, we risk confusing correlation with causality.

Many variables affect health in addition to the provision of health care: air and water quality, diet, smoking, exercise, speed limits, availability of firearms, etc. Nonetheless, with such large sums being invested in health care, we must examine the rough measures that do exist and infer cautiously about health system effectiveness.

Basic to any examination of health outcomes is a consideration of life expectancy. Over the past three decades, life expectancy has been increasing at similar rates in Japan, Canada, Germany, the United Kingdom, and the United States. This increase has been seen in both men and women, although women live approximately 5 years longer than men in each nation. It should be noted, however, that the United States lags slightly behind the other nations in terms of life expectancy.

Over the same period, infant mortality has declined, steeply at first and then more gradually. Again, the United States fares somewhat worse than the comparator nations. General population mortality performance is mixed, but falls within a fairly tight range (figure 4). Approximately two-thirds of all deaths in each nation arise from the top two major causes: heart

Figure 4. Infant Mortality in Five Industrialized Nations, 1960–1998

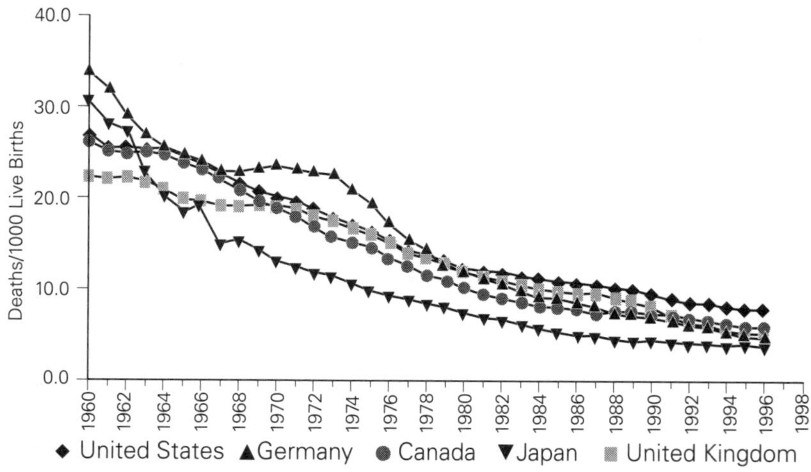

Source: OECD Health Data 1998

disease and cancer (figure 5).

On balance, what is striking about the health outcomes of the systems in these five countries is their similarity. Health, as it can be measured, has been improving. Spending, too, has been increasing. Also, although people are living longer, they are dying of similar causes and at similar rates.

Why are health care costs so much higher in the United States than in other developed nations? There are many possible reasons. Perhaps it is because, per capita, the United States provides more care (as measured by the number or duration of doctor visits, hospital stays, or prescriptions). In addition, the United States may be providing higher-cost care at similar rates per capita. We also may be delivering health care less efficiently (i.e., with high administrative or overhead costs). Another explanation may be that the costs of other health systems are being "externalized," that is, expenses are taking the form of long patient-waiting times and unnecessary suffering.

Analysis of existing data suggests that higher U.S. health care expenditures are driven by higher per-unit cost of care. Hospital expenses are the largest component of health care spending, about 40 percent of the total. U.S. hospitals have fewer beds and shorter lengths of stay, but employ more staff and technology to accomplish the job.

Figure 5. Mortality in Five Industrialized Nations, 1960–1998

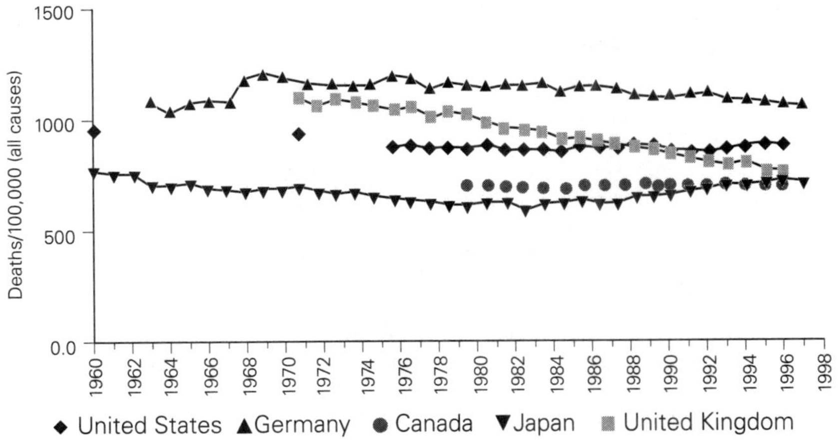

Source: OECD Health Data 1998

Physician services make up the second biggest health system expense, comprising approximately 20 percent of the total. The United States has a high number of physicians, and they are among the highest paid. Nevertheless, they see their patients no more frequently than do their international colleagues (figure 6).

How do other nations control the cost per unit of service? The details vary by country, but the broad answer is that powerful associations of payers (national or state government, insurance companies, or sickness funds) bargain with providers over fee schedules or institutional budgets. With most care covered within this framework, little opportunity exists for the cost to shift backward to payers, forward to patients, or sideways to other payers. In such budgetary systems, controls are often mandated (or adopted by administrators) to prevent the proliferation of expensive technology or growth in physician supply.

ACADEMIC HEALTH CENTER LESSONS: A CASE STUDY IN WASTED RESOURCES

One might argue that, short of a major national reform of health care, aca-

Figure 6. Average Physician Visits in Five Industrialized Nations, 1998

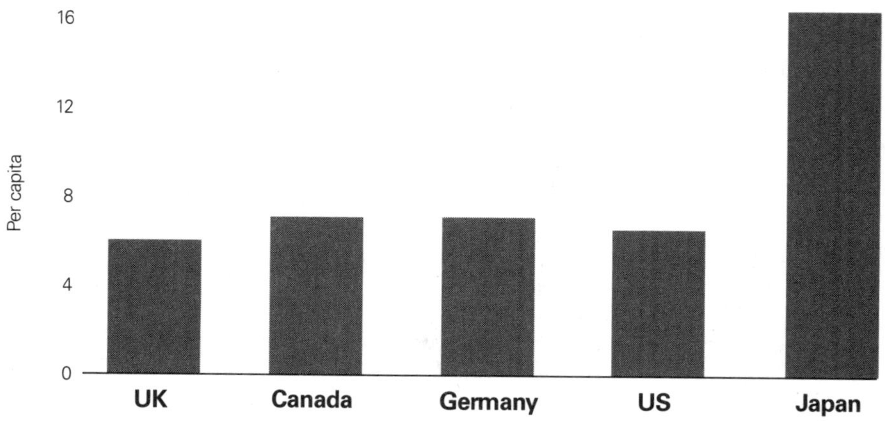

Source: OECD Health Data 1998

demic health centers in the United States can do little to learn from the international experience. This view, however, is mistaken. Indeed, the authors' experience within a large academic health center also proves otherwise.

As previously noted, many nations (other than Japan) keep costs down in part by maintaining tight controls on capital equipment expenditures (i.e., outlays for long-term assets that are expensed over many years). At times and in certain countries, difficult choices made to constrain such spending have produced waiting lists for nonemergency procedures or a preference for lower-cost, lower-resolution imaging.

The United States, on the other hand, may have the opposite problem: an oversupply of sophisticated technology. Some might argue that this is the unavoidable result of hospital competition, or what is often called the "medical arms race." Although true during the Cold War years, the basis for competition in health care (and, coincidentally, between the United States and Russia) has changed drastically in the last decade.

Technological competition is still a factor for academic health centers, but it is only one of many explanations for the oversupply of sophisticated medical technology. Consider the following typical anecdote that any external health care consultant (such as the coauthors) can relate.

An analysis of Radiology Department data at a large institution recently indicated that, of 150 different imaging machines, 60 were being used once per day or less. When queried, organizational managers and radiologists reacted defensively, suggesting that these results could be explained by inappropriate data entry (a poor use of expensive information technology), special research and teaching needs, and the failure to retire old and fully depreciated resources. These justifications indeed were true to some extent. Nonetheless, it was also true that the department capital was not being managed efficiently. Many seldom-used resources took up rooms full of expensive (and highly needed) space, and all the machinery required maintenance or service contracts as well as a spare-parts inventory. Erroneously assuming that all resources were being used at full capacity, administrators were continuing to replace equipment.

We discovered, as might be expected, that the process by which hospital capital expenditures were approved was political. The powerful won the day. This statement is less pejorative than realistic. The world is political. Once we face this fact, we can seriously consider the character of political processes. Does the political process weed out the truly bad ideas despite the power of their advocates? Does it allow the good ideas to bubble up, even from weak advocates?

At this particular academic health center, department managers and clinical chiefs, armed with cost-benefit reports, argued with the hospital's top officers in favor of their department's priorities. Anyone familiar with such constructions knows that, in such situations, people tend to project great future benefits (often with help from the vendors) while understating the costs. Surprisingly, the Finance Department's role at this institution was to support these analyses, not question them.

What this institution was missing was an organizational force that questions the assumptions of such reports and holds the managers accountable for the benefits promised once the money is spent. In this case, by the time the funds were spent, the original analyses had found the dustbin. Promised benefits, which often had necessitated painful labor cuts or procedural changes, typically failed to materialize. This pattern is by no means unique to the particular academic health center used as an example. Every institution should develop such an organizational force to control costs.

Those charged with the responsibility of controlling costs must have access to the data used to make cost-and-benefit projections. The members of this force also need the analytical skills to make sense of the data, as well as an appreciation for the clinical processes to be funded. In addition, it would be wise to give the force members tenure or some other form of job security, so that frustrated project advocates cannot undermine their careers.

Tighter management of capital expenditures will become increasingly important as the health care industry invests more heavily in information technology (IT). Other industries, better known for their management expertise, have been frustrated with their returns on such investments. Other nations have strong IT cost controls in place. The wise academic health center executive will learn from these other countries and carefully examine the organization's capacity to choose and manage these large investments. This is a case of the aforementioned form of lesson-drawing that is rare but powerful: a policy generalization that holds true in many divergent cases, across all countries.

HEALTH POLICY, NATIONAL SCHEMES, AND GLOBAL FORCES

Why is health reform a global trend today? Health care policy came to the forefront of public agendas during the late 1980s and early 1990s for one or more of the following reasons.

First, all around the world, the financing of personal health care had become a major financial component of the budgets for mature welfare states. When fiscal strain arises, as it did during the prolonged recession of recent years, the predictable result is policy scrutiny, not simply incremental budgeting.

Second, under almost all circumstances, mature welfare states have less capacity for bold fiscal expansion in new areas (O'Higgins and Klein, 1988). This means that the management of existing programs (in new ways perhaps, but under changing economic circumstances) necessarily occupies a larger share of the public agenda. We also are now seeing what might be termed the "wearing out" (or perhaps the "wearing down") of the postwar consensus about the welfare state—namely, we are at last outgrowing the effects of more than two decades of fretfulness about the affordability, desirability, and governability of the welfare state (Murray, 1995; Herrnstein, Murray, 1996).

The critics of welfare became outspoken during the 1973-74 oil crisis when they were sustained by stagflation and bolstered by the advance of parties opposed to welfare state expansion. For the first time, the mass public witnessed programs being challenged that for decades had seemed sacrosanct (Marmor et al., 1990). From Mulroney to Thatcher, and from New Zealand to the Netherlands, reformers were calling for a "necessary change."

At such times, when economic strain reappears, the inner rim of programmatic protection weakens, that is, not because the commitment of particular interest groups grows more faint but because their social faith dwindles. The incentives for exploring transformative, but fiscally practical options, grow stronger. Such developments help to explain the clear international pattern of welfare state review, including health policy, over the past decade. It is a process of review that intensified in 1990 as recession moved across national borders.

CONCLUSION

Even if we accept this contention, however, the question still remains: Why have these reviews focused so much attention on other national experiences? Times of policy change sharply increase the demand for new ideas, or at least for new means to old ends. Just as many U.S. analysts have turned to Canada's example, so too have Canadian, German, Dutch, and other analysts turned their attention internationally. This is readily seen at international meetings where conference participants eagerly cite accounts from other countries' experiences.

As illustration, let us consider the topics in which attendees expressed interest at one recent international conference. Participants sought to obtain better policy answers to the problems conferees face at home, such as how to find a balance between solidarity and subsidiarity; how to maintain a high-quality health system in times of economic stress; and (an optimistic query) what are the optimum relations between patients, insurers, providers, and the government.

If viewed as simple expressions of curiosity, these topics are comparatively unremarkable. However, if the topics are understood to be an outgrowth of a diligent pursuit of the best health care model (albeit excluding further exploration of the political, social, and economic context required for implementation), they reveal an overall intent to initiate change, even if the intention constitutes little more than wishful thinking. This is a crucial distinction because all too often conferees see international meetings as an opportunity to exchange information merely so they can stretch themselves intellectually. In such a case, people may embark upon quests to exchange policy information of various sorts without intending to make a commitment to policy importation. In other words, there is a substantial difference between simply exchanging views with kindred spirits and explicitly seeking to stimulate new ideas about specific initiatives.

What may be said about drawing policy lessons from such international conferences? What are the rules of defensible conduct at these meetings, and are they followed? The truth is that, whatever the appearances, most policy debates in most countries are, and will remain, parochial affairs. They address national problems and emphasize historical and contemporary national developments within a particular domain (pensions, medical finance, transportation, etc.). In general, they embody conflicting visions of which policies each particular country should adopt. Only rarely do participants seriously consider the experiences of other nations and the lessons they can teach.

Unfortunately, when cross-national comparisons are employed in such parochial struggles, their use is typically limited to policy warfare and not to policy understanding and careful lesson-drawing. Furthermore, at home there are typically few knowledgeable critics of ideas about solutions abroad. In the world of the U.S. health care debate, the misuse of the British and Canadian experience surely illustrates this point. From the late 1940s to the late 1970s, the U.K. National Health Service was viewed by many U.S. observers as the specter of what government medicine and rationing could mean. In recent years, mythmaking about Canada has dominated the distortion league tables in North America (Marmor, 1994). It is clear that the parochialism of national debates remains dominant.

The reasons are almost too obvious to cite. Policy makers and managers are busy with day-to-day pressures. If they take the time for comparative inquiry at all, practical concerns incline them to pay more attention to what appears to work. They cannot take the time to examine academic reasons for what is and is not transferable, and why.

Policy debaters, whether they are politicians, policy analysts, or representatives of particular interest groups, are more engaged in struggles than in seminars. Like trial lawyers, they seek victory, not illumination. For this purpose, compelling stories, whether well-substantiated or not, seem to be more useful than careful conclusions. Interest groups, as their label suggests, have material and symbolic stakes in policy outcomes and neither have nor feel the need to protect a reputation for intellectual precision.

These considerations are not new, nor are they surprising. However, there has been an increased flow of cross-national claims in health policy in recent years. This trend, if nothing else, will generate new reasons to reconsider the meaning of cross-national policy learning.

REFERENCES

Herrnstein RJ, Murray C. 1996. *The Bell Curve: Intelligence and Class Structure in American Life.* New York, NY: The Free Press.

Marmor, TR. 1994. Patterns of Fact and Fiction in United States of the Canadian Experience. In *Understanding Health Care Reform.* New Haven, CT: Yale University Press, p.185.

Marmor TR, Mashaw J, and Harvey P. 1990. *America's Misunderstood Welfare State: Persistent Myths, Enduring Realities.* New York, NY: Basic Book Publishers.

Murray C. 1995. *Losing Ground.* New York, NY: Basic Books.

O'Higgins M, and Klein R. 1988. Audit in medical practice, *Journal of Medical Science,* 157(4):99.

OECD (Organization for Economic Co-Operation and Development). 1998. *OECD Health Data 1998: A Comparative Analysis of 29 Countries.* Washington, DC: Brookings Institution Press.

Schieber G, Maeda A. 1999. Health Care Financing and Delivery in Developing Countries. *Health Affairs,* 18(3) 193-205.

5. India's Hard-Won Lessons

VULIMIRI RAMALINGASWAMI

DURING THE SECOND HALF OF THE 20TH CENTURY, India learned a number of lessons the hard way about health care and health development. By observing and learning from India's mistakes, we can develop a better perspective on the global dimensions of health and international health reform.

When India became independent of British rule in 1947, it already had in hand the 1946 report of the Health Survey and Development Committee, popularly known as the Bhore Committee Report, after the committee's chairman, Sir Joseph Bhore. (India Health Survey and Development Committee, 1946). The Bhore Report was monumental. Its impact upon health care in India was akin to the Flexner Report's influence early in the century upon academic medicine in the industrialized world (Flexner, 1910). Indeed, the Flexner and Bhore reports, although separate in time, complement each other well. Together, they constitute a nearly complete program of health reform.

Note: This paper is based upon the John R. Hogness Lecture delivered by the author at the 1999 annual meeting of the Association of Academic Health Centers.

The Bhore Report, which focused upon extending health services to India's districts and beyond, served as a blueprint for health development in the newly independent India. India's health program, implemented through a series of successive 5-year plans, was in many ways a precursor to the modern-day Declaration of Alma-Ata.

LOSING DIRECTION AFTER A STRONG START

Our country was blessed with these advantages at its birth. However, somewhere along the road to health, India seems to have lost its direction. Granted, we have had significant successes, such as the substantial reductions in the infant mortality rate, significant increases in life expectancy at birth, and marked reductions in crude death rates (Central Health Education Bureau, 1998). In addition, India's ability to deal with famines has vastly improved: Our people no longer die as a result of famine. We have eradicated smallpox and guineaworm disease. We are in the final stages of eliminating iodine deficiency diseases. Polio is fast diminishing, thanks to the implementation of National Immunization Days, a situation particularly vital to global health, for unless India is free from polio, the world will not be free from polio.

This health transition has been accompanied by a transition in India's demographics. During the 1980s and 1990s, the number of Indians above age 70 increased by 102 percent (Ramalingaswami, 1997). Beginning in the year 2000, India will have approximately 75.7 million people above the age of 60.

On balance, however, many failures mar the health landscape in India. With each new 5-year plan, targets of disease control and fertility control continue to shift. Given all of India's strengths, the general impression is that India is an underachiever in health care.

THE ROOT(S) OF THE PROBLEM

What is at the root of India's poor to modest performance in health? I believe they are operational inefficiency, poor management, and inadequate policy formulation. The most striking management paradox can be found in the field of nutrition: India has made substantial contributions to a better understanding of nutritional disorders worldwide. Our pilot projects have demonstrated successful control of nutritional disorders. Nonetheless, India, which is home to less than 20 percent of the world's child population, has almost 40 percent of all the malnourished children in the world. Fifty percent of South Asia's children are malnourished. Half of the malnourished children around the globe are located in India, Bangladesh, and Pakistan.

Low birth weight is a good predictor of overall health status. Approximately one-third of all newborns in India weigh less than 2.5 kilograms. This statistic has not improved over the years. In South Asia, 33 percent of all newborns are low birth weight, in comparison with 18 percent for developing countries as a whole. Closely connected to the problem of low birth weight is the issue of nutrition. South Asia's nutrition is the worst in the world, worse even than in sub-Saharan Africa. South Asia is fast emerging as the poorest, most illiterate, most malnourished, least gender-sensitive, and indeed most deprived region in the world.

Add to this situation the increasing evidence supporting Professor David Barker's hypothesis that fetal malnutrition (which is manifested as low birth weight) predisposes a child to developing a number of prevalent adult diseases later in life, including hypertension, coronary heart disease, diabetes, and even breast cancer (Begley, 1999). The link between low birth weight and cardiovascular disease is also emerging as one of the strongest elements in fetal programming. Low birth weight is increasingly being identified as a marker for a complex set of factors influencing fetal growth and susceptibility to disease in later life. Indeed, low birth weight may be seen as a whole new paradigm in public health. According to Begley's article, we may have gone overboard in ascribing traits exclusively to genes. Meanwhile, we may have underplayed the effects of ones environment. Having a gene for a particular trait does not necessarily mean that the trait will be manifested; the gene must be activated in order to exert its effect. In light of this, good nutrition in anticipation of pregnancy (i.e., during adolescence and in the preconceptional period) becomes pivotal in promoting public health.

Practitioners in the medical and nutritional sciences know what needs to be done to end malnutrition; those in the social sciences know how to implement antimalnutrition programs. The fields must come together in order to banish the ills caused by malnutrition. Unfortunately, India has failed to coordinate these fields or to make use of its own scientists' knowledge. Neither has it utilized the available technologies, which are well known and proven to be effective.

WINNING AND LOSING THE BATTLE AGAINST COMMUNICABLE DISEASES

For the most part, India's successes have been in the field of communicable diseases. In the late 1950s and 1960s, our nation was a showpiece for malaria control. During this time, not a single death from malaria was reported throughout the country. In addition, by spraying DDT for malaria control, India also eliminated the sandfly, vector of visceral leishmaniasis, or Kala-azar.

Sadly, however, these successes were not sustained. Both malaria and Kala-azar have returned in India; there have been serious outbreaks of both diseases (Ramalingaswami, 1996). In addition, plague—which had disappeared from India for over three decades—returned in 1994 with an outbreak of both the pneumonic and bubonic forms in parts of Gujarat and Maharashtra. The return of Plague caused much suffering, as well as an estimated loss of US$ 1.7 billion in trade (Ramalingaswami, 1995; Panda, Nanda, Ghosh et al., 1996). One of India's toughest challenges in dealing with the recent outbreak of Plague was the absence of medical practitioners with an institutional memory of the disease.

Plague is by no means the only disease that is rearing its head in India. India is now a crucible of emerging and reemerging infections. HIV/AIDS, which is spreading at a rapid rate, is moving out of high-risk areas into the general population, including rural areas. Today, approximately 3.5 million people in India are known to be infected with HIV.

In addition, a devastating form of Dengue hemorrhagic fever has spread to India from the Far East. Over the years, Japanese encephalitis has evolved from sporadic, endemic cases to large-scale outbreaks. Today it causes many deaths and much disability. Leptospirosis outbreaks also are causing great concern in several parts of India, including the Andaman and Nicobar Islands. Malaria now occupies distinct ecological niches throughout the country, and falciparum malaria is on the rise. The fires of Kala-azar are still burning in the plains of Bihar, as well as in the adjoining areas of Uttar Pradesh, West Bengal, and Assam.

There is no doubt that "the restless tide" of infectious diseases is now a global phenomenon. The recent appearance of West Nile encephalitis in New York City serves as a grim reminder of this phenomenon foretold years ago by Dr. Richard Krause (1981) in his visionary book, The Restless Tide.

A number of lessons can be drawn from the Indian experience. India's problems can be traced in part, to an inability to sustain success that is tied, in turn, to the complacency into which its health care program fell following the initial wave of successes. In addition, a variety of well-meant developmental activities created environmental conditions conducive to vector proliferation. They include the irrigation and infrastructural construction projects for communication and buildings that altered land and water use. The lesson to be learned is that a country needs to foresee the environmental impact of its developmental activities before embarking upon them. Potential dangers must be assessed and appropriate preventive measures taken. Ecological integrity and economic growth can, and must, function compatibly.

THE MISSING LINKS IN INDIA'S PUBLIC HEALTH PROGRAM

In India, there is a dichotomy between the fields of science and health, and it takes the form of a failure to couple knowledge to action. The history of health development in today's industrialized countries tells us that basic health technologies such as safe water, sanitation, personal hygiene, food availability, and education have brought about remarkable strides in public health. These technologies created a transformation in health during the first Industrial Revolution, well before the magic bullets of modern medicine came into being.

Some progress has been made in introducing these basic health technologies to the developing world through the United Nations and other national and international agencies. However, there is still a backlog of needs; international agencies are unable to apply these basic health techniques universally.

In light of this, it should be clear that securing the benefits of science for all people requires taking action on a multisectoral front in a coordinated manner. Promoting global health requires engaging a genuine political will. It means giving recipients and providers of care the proper education so they will remain motivated to implement basic health technologies. It involves stirring people to action in a spirit of self-care and self-help. It demands the use of the technologies that are cost effective, accessible, and acceptable within the socioeconomic milieu of those in greatest need.

Often the key determinants of health lie outside the health sector: water, sanitation, environment, agriculture, housing, industrial development, transport, and tourism. Health-promoting activities in these diverse sectors must work together synergistically. They may be the loci of the missing links in India's public health program. Our country did not implement intersectoral approaches nor did it form effective partnerships with individual communities.

It is vital that we overcome complacency with regard to diseases that we consider to be conquered. Thirty years free of plague, India was caught unprepared for the recent outbreaks. Now, fortunately, India has established a National Infectious Diseases Surveillance and Response system. This system integrates public health laboratory services, epidemiologic capabilities, and epidemic preparedness. It also is strengthening the country's ability to couple immediate response to surveillance data.

In addition, we are developing a system for disease surveillance at the district level (John et al., 1998). Clues to impending outbreaks may be found in ecological disturbances, heavy rainfall, and rise in vector population densities. Public health cannot be advanced without having such a surveillance and response mechanism in place.

Another lesson that India has learned through bitter experience is that, in dealing with infectious diseases, time is of the essence. This was well illustrated by the outbreak of tuberculosis (TB) many years ago. In the wake of that outbreak, India's Tuberculosis Research Centre in Madras established controlled clinical trials as a major instrument for advancing evidence-based medicine and public health. Today, evidence-based medicine is our paradigm for medical care. We need to base all health initiatives and preventive medicine programs firmly upon sound scientific evidence (Woolf et al., 1996).

India's TB Research Centre played a critical role in demonstrating the efficacy of multidrug therapy against TB on a domiciliary basis. The center drew up an excellent blueprint for national TB control, and the sanitoria were closed. Many other countries adopted this plan and have achieved remarkable success in controlling the disease.

However, in regard to its conquest of TB, India once again failed to couple knowledge to action. Despite having had a quarter-century of lead time in which to implement effective chemotherapy (and despite demonstrating the efficacy of supervised treatments to ensure compliance long before direct observed therapies came on the scene), India today is no longer on the front line battling TB. Indeed, this slippage has cost the nation dearly when a drug resistant strain of TB developed. In addition, the advent of HIV/AIDS in 1988 further enhanced the spread of TB. (How fortunate that smallpox was eradicated before the emergence of HIV/AIDS!) The tragedy of TB in India is that, although highly effective therapy that was available for years, it was not used as effectively as it could have been. As a result, more people now suffer from TB than at any previous period of human history (Grange and Zumla, 1997).

However, there is hope for the future in the promise of preventive vaccines, shortened chemotherapies, and highly sensitive diagnostic tests. All of these remedies will be made possible by the sequencing of the M. tuberculosis genome (Pym and Cole, 1999). It is symbolic of the new link between basic science and public health.

Epidemiology can also act as a key link between medicine and public health. One example is the International Clinical Epidemiology Network (INCLEN), initiated with great vision by the Rockefeller Foundation. INCLEN trains clinical researchers, social scientists, statisticians, and health economists from selected academic institutions in developing countries. Its program enhances interdisciplinary and international collaboration, thereby helping to bring the ideal of global health within reach.

In India, clinical care, the community, and health all function in watertight compartments. As in many other countries, the dominant ethos continues to be an emphasis upon disease-based care rather than a focus upon wider public health efforts. This outlook, however, is changing elsewhere: For instance, the latest White Paper in England advocates the introduction of cardiac defibrillators in public places (Secretary of State for Health, 1999), an issue also debated in the United States. It is an excellent example of bringing clinical care and public health together in a holistic relationship. In this way, we can restore the continuum of disease care, disease prevention, and health promotion.

THE ACADEMIC SIDE: LOSING TOUCH WITH PUBLIC HEALTH

The recent, spectacular advances in clinical medicine, compounded by the new dimension of molecular science, act naturally as a magnet for young physicians. Students in medical training now opt more and more for clinical specialization and super-specialization. As intriguing as this may be, the unfortunate result is that many academic health centers in India are losing their focus upon community health at the undergraduate and postgraduate levels. As proof, it is remarkable to note that India has more than 160 medical colleges, yet only 2 or 3 schools of public health. The basic disciplines of epidemiology, biostatistics, human variation, human behavior, health economics, health-related social sciences, health policy and programming, surveillance and response, and health outcome measurement are not flourishing.

The great Indian paradox (the lack of congruence between scientific capability and public health advances) cannot be substantially addressed until this glaring deficiency is rectified. We will be on the road to an effective health care program only when we are producing adequate numbers of high-quality public health officials, and when the prevention of disease and the promotion and maintenance of health are given equal status with the diagnosis, prognosis, and treatment of disease.

A great apostle of peace, nonviolence, and ethics noted long ago the importance of prevention:

> *I am hard-hearted enough to let the sick die, if you can tell me how to prevent others from falling sick.*
>
> —Mahatma Gandhi

REFERENCES

Association of Academic Health Centers. 1999. *Celebrating 30 years: 1999 Annual Report.* Washington, DC: AHC.

Begley S. Shaped by life in the womb. 1999. *Newsweek,* Sept 27:50-57.

Central Health Education Bureau, Directorate-General of Health Services. 1998. 50 years of Health and Family Welfare: Special issue of *Swasth Hind.* New Delhi, India: Ministry of Health and Family Welfare, January, 176.

Flexner, A. 1910. *Medical Education in the United States and Canada.* New York, NY: Carnegie Foundation for the Advancement of Teaching.

Grange J and Zumla A. 1997. Tuberculosis: An epidemic of injustice. *Journal of the Royal College of Physicians of London,* 31(6):637-638.

India Health Survey and Development Committee. 1946. *Report.* Delhi: Manager of Publications.

John TJ, Reuben S, Balraj V, and John R. 1998. Disease surveillance at district level: A model for developing countries. *Lancet,* 352:58-61.

Krause R. *The Restless Tide.* 1981. Washington, DC: National Foundation for Infectious Diseases.

Panda SK, Nanda SK, Ghosh A, Sharma C, Shivaji S, Seshu Kumar G, Kannan K, Batra HV, Tuteja U, Ganguly NK, Chakraborty A, Sharat A, and Chandra S. 1996. The 1994 plague epidemic in India: Molecular diagnosis and characterization of Yersinia pestis isolates from Surat and Beed. *Current Science,* 71(10):794-799.

Pym AS and Cole ST. 1999. Post-DOTS, post genomics: The next century of tuberculosis control. *Lancet,* 353 (March 2):1004-1005.

Ramalingaswami V. 1995. Resurgence of diseases once under control: Now the Plague. *Proceedings of the Indian National Science Academy,* 1995; B(61)4:241-248.

——. 1996. Infectious diseases in a changing world. *Current Science,* 70:1050-1056.

——. 1997. Aging. *National Medical Journal of India,* 10(5):235-236.

Secretary of State for Health. 1999. *Saving Lives: Our Healthier Nation.* London: The Stationery Office.

Woolf SH, Di Guiseppi CG, Atkins D, and Kamerow DB. 1996. Developing evidenced-based clinical practice guidelines: Lessons learned by the 4S Preventive Services Task Force. *Annual Review of Public Health,* 17:511-538.

TECHNOLOGY FOR GOOD AND EVIL

6. *Infectious Disease and the Threat Of Bioterrorism*

JAMES M. HUGHES

INFECTIOUS DISEASES ARE THE LEADING CAUSE OF death worldwide today, accounting for approximately one-third of the global burden of mortality. What people often forget, however, is that infectious diseases also are a significant cause of mortality in the United States. A recent examination of trends in the United States during the 20th century revealed a decrease in infectious disease mortality through the century up until 1980, after which it rose and has continued to rise through 1995 (Armstrong, Conn, Pinner, 1999).

MICROBIAL WAKE-UP CALLS

We have had a number of recent wake-up calls regarding the emergence and reemergence of infectious diseases, thanks in large part to a landmark Institute of Medicine report (Lederberg, Shope, Oaks, 1992). It revealed that the complacency in this country (and in a number of other developed countries) throughout the 1970s and 1980s was based upon the misconception that infectious diseases were finally under control. The report also identified new, reemerging, or drug-resistant infections that have increased within the past two decades or whose incidence threatens to increase in the near future. Six factors contribute to this situation:

1. Changes in human demographics and behavior.
2. Advances in technology and industry.
3. Economic development and changes in land use patterns.
4. Dramatic expansion in the volume and the speed of international travel and commerce, which has exponentially increased the movement of people, animals, foods, and other commodities around the world.
5. The unique ability of microbes to constantly evolve in response to selective pressures in their environment.
6. The failure of public health measures to address infectious diseases at the local, state, national, and even international levels. This breakdown in the public health system comes into play whether one is dealing with naturally occurring diseases or those that are introduced intentionally.

Since 1993, the Centers for Disease Control and Prevention (CDC) has put considerable emphasis on strengthening the national capacity to deal with emerging infectious diseases. In 1994, we published an initial CDC Emerging Infectious Plan (CDC, 1994) and updated it in late 1998 (CDC, 1998). In the plan's fourfold strategy, which also relates directly to bioterrorism, the CDC commits to:

- Strengthen surveillance and response capacity.
- Upgrade applied research to address the many questions raised by these emerging infectious diseases.
- Strengthen prevention and control programs.
- Develop an infrastructure and training programs.*

It is difficult to predict the future, but it is reasonably certain that in the

* The 1998 plan emphasizes the importance of training a workforce adequate for dealing with infectious disease issues in the clinical, laboratory, and public health settings.

coming years we will continue to be challenged by antimicrobial resistance at the local, national, and global levels. We face the continuing threat of the next influenza pandemic. There have been three in this century, and the last occurred in 1968–69. We also will continue to experience a wide range of national and international food-borne diseases.

Microbes also may play a role in a wide range of chronic diseases. Several recent studies indicate that infections, and particularly infections involving Chlamydia pneumoniae, may play a role in causing or accelerating the progression of atherosclerosis.

We also need to be prepared to confront the unexpected, such as the outbreak of avian influenza in Hong Kong. Fortunately, avian influenza was not a strain that was transmitted readily from person to person. Still it was yet another wake-up call in terms of the threat of pandemic influenza. More recently in Malaysia and Singapore, there was a complex outbreak, affecting both pigs and people, caused by a previously unrecognized paramyxovirus, known now as Nipah virus. And in the United States, we have had the recent outbreak of a West Nile-like virus causing encephalitis in New York City and surrounding areas.

From these national and international outbreaks, we have learned the importance of surveillance. Once a problem is detected, it is critical that a country have the epidemiologic capacity to conduct a timely and prompt investigation. It is equally critical that researchers have access to modern, sophisticated public health laboratories. Already, we have witnessed the disruption of travel and commerce that can be caused by these complex outbreaks. Today, local outbreaks have potentially global implications. We also have learned that the level of media interest often is inversely proportional to the overall magnitude of a disease.

BIOTERRORISM: WHEN SUSPENSE NOVELS COME TRUE

Another dimension of this health scenario is the threat of bioterrorism. Many readers may be familiar with a popular novel by Richard Preston, *The Cobra Event.* It is a fictionalized account of an episode of bioterrorism in New York City (Preston 1997). People often wonder, Is this scenario realistic? Is bioterrorism a genuine threat?

It is both. In fact, bioterrorism already has taken place in the United States. (There also have been hoaxes, such as the package reputedly containing infectious disease microbes that was mailed to B'nai Brith headquarters in Washington, D.C.) However, in 1984, there was a documented case of bioterrorism in the small town of The Dalles, Oregon, a community outbreak of salmonellosis was traced to the intentional contamination of restaurant salad bars by members of the Rajneesh Sect who were conducting a pilot test in preparation for their plans to disrupt a local election. There were more than 750 documented cases of culture-confirmed *salmonella typhimurium* infection. After a long investigation, researchers identified salad bars in ten different restaurants throughout town as the mode of disease transmission. A criminal investigation subsequently identified the bioterrorists as the followers of the Bhagwan Shree Rajneesh (Torok et al., 1997).

This threat of bioterrorism, even more than the threat of emerging infectious diseases, demands that we form new partnerships and strengthen existing relationships within the health care community. Professionals in the clinical medicine and public health sectors need to collaborate to combat this problem, just as they need to collaborate in fighting antimicrobial resistance, food-borne diseases, and the many other emerging issues in the field of infectious diseases. In the case of bioterrorism, collaboration also must include emergency response personnel, Federal agencies, law enforcement agencies, and the intelligence community. The Clinton Administration has recognized bioterrorism as a legitimate threat to our society. In his commencement address at the U.S. Naval Academy, President Clinton (1998) declared that we need to address this threat as a national security priority. He subsequently issued Presidential directives instructing Federal agencies to work together to address these issues (Clinton 1999).

When considering the threat of bioterrorism, we tend to focus on a core group of agents, including the organisms or toxins that cause anthrax, botulism, brucellosis, plague, Q fever, smallpox, staphylococcal food-borne disease, tularemia, the viral encephalitides (particularly Venezuelan equine encephalitis), and potentially some of the viral hemorrhagic fevers. However, as the episode in Oregon demonstrates, there is a broad range of other microbial pathogens that also can be used by bioterrorists, including the organisms that cause cholera, salmonellosis, and shigellosis.

Why does the threat of bioterrorism pose such a great problem? Since most physicians have seen very few cases of infection caused by the organisms in the core group, they have very little familiarity with most of these diseases. In addition, our population has little or no immunity against most of these diseases. Until very recently, there has been little, if any, active research conducted on most of these diseases.

ARE WE PREPARED FOR A BIOLOGICAL ATTACK?

Because of the incubation period associated with infectious diseases, it is the frontline health care providers (emergency medical workers, personnel in outpatient clinics and critical care units, and practitioners dealing with infection control) who will be the first to deal with patients who may have been infected as a result of an intentional release. There is a significant delay between a victim's exposure to infectious elements and the experience of symptoms. This is in direct contrast to a chemical event, such as the release of sarin in the Tokyo subway, in which victims immediately collapsed at the site of exposure.

Symptoms of bioterrorism may be difficult to identify, particularly given the broad spectrum of illnesses that might be involved: encephalitis, hemorrhagic mediastinitis (the most likely presenting condition of anthrax), pneumonia with abnormal liver function tests (a clue to Q fever), papulopustular rash (an indication of smallpox, which could well be the worst disaster of all), descending symmetrical paralysis (possibly indicating botulism), hemorrhagic fever, and simple nausea, vomiting, or diarrhea (which might suggest exposure to a staphylococcal enterotoxin). The most difficult problem with all these conditions is that very few of the symptoms are specific enough to be readily identified, except possibly the hemorrhagic mediastinitis associated with anthrax and the papulopustular rash potentially associated with smallpox.

How might these diseases be disseminated? Since the preferred means of spreading disease is likely to be by inhalation, bioterrorists are most likely to use aerosols as the medium of infection. Infected food, water, or vectors also could be used. These vehicles are more likely to be contaminated with a chemical rather than a biological toxin. There also is the possibility of contamination through oral or intravenous medications.

What is the status of vaccines for the diseases most likely to be used in bioterrorism? Unfortunately, our armamentarium of vaccines is not extensive. We do have licensed vaccines for anthrax, plague, and smallpox, but they are difficult to obtain and unavailable in large quantities. Additionally, under our nation's Investigational New Drug (IND) arrangements, we have vaccines against botulism, Q fever, tularemia, and Venezuelan equine encephalitis.

The Institute of Medicine recently issued a thorough report focusing on research and development issues related to preparedness for biological and chemical terrorism within the civilian and medical communities (Institute of Medicine, 1999). This report concluded that the medical community, including public health agencies, emergency medical services, hospitals, and health care providers, would bear the brunt of a chemical or biological attack. This is an issue that is directly relevant to the members of the Association of Academic Health Centers. President Clinton (1999) called attention to this particular threat at the National Academy of Sciences in the context of his budget request for bioterrorism and chemical terrorism preparedness.

In terms of the public health response to bioterrorism, the issues are similar to those related to emerging infections: the need for early detection, prompt investigation and response, and rapid diagnosis. We will need to know the diseases with which we are dealing, and we will need to have a rapid communication system in place (an issue that often is overlooked in the more typical outbreak of infectious diseases) if we are to disseminate information efficiently to both the general public and the professionals who will be dealing with the problem.

In the FY1999 CDC appropriation, $121.8 million was earmarked in the following categories:

- $4.8 million for planning.
- $38 million for surveillance, epidemiology, and laboratory capacity.
- $28 million for a communications system linking state and local health departments, using modern communications technology (an investment that is long overdue).

- $51 million for a pharmaceutical and drug stockpile to accumulate vaccines, drugs, and other supplies that would be necessary in the event of a major crisis.

A substantial proportion of the nonstockpile funds have been awarded extramurally to state and local health departments in five categories:

1. Preparedness, planning, and readiness assessment.
2. Surveillance and epidemiology capacity building.
3. Laboratory capacity building, with emphasis on biological agents.
4. Laboratory capacity building, with emphasis on chemical agents.
5. Development of a communications network and the associated training.

At CDC, we also are taking steps to increase our own internal laboratory and epidemiologic capacity. The Epidemic Intelligence Service, CDC's 2-year training program, founded in 1951 to give physicians and others interested in public health practical experience in this area, was justified in part by the threat of bioterrorism during the Korean War. Since then, we have placed additional emphasis on creating a rapid diagnostic laboratory, developing and maintaining the national drug and device stockpile, meeting training needs, and administering the Select Agent Rule, a law passed by Congress to decrease access by potential perpetrators to microbial and chemical agents that could be used in bioterrorism.

In June 1999, the United States opposed the planned destruction of the smallpox virus. Destruction has been postponed for at least 3 years so that additional research can be conducted on the virus. In a recent editorial in *Science,* Secretary of Health and Human Services Donna Shalala (1999) enumerated the reasons for this decision, as well as the Clinton Administration's priorities for a research and development program.

There are several other references that readers may choose to review to get a comprehensive overview on the subject of bioterrorism. In 1997, a special issue of *The Journal of the American Medical Association* contained a complete account of what is known about bioterrorism and what has happened in the past in terms of biological warfare and terrorism (American Medical Association, 1997). A 1999 issue of the CDC journal, *Emerging Infectious Diseases,* contains the proceedings of a very timely conference organized by the Johns Hopkins Center for Civilian Biodefense Studies in February 1999 (Centers for Disease Control and Prevention, 1999).

As President Clinton said in his address to the National Academy of Sciences in January 1999,

> These cutting-edge efforts targeted toward bioterrorism preparedness will address not only the threat of weapons of mass destruction, but also the equally serious danger of emerging infectious diseases.

One cannot overemphasize the importance and complementarity of improving both our preparedness for bioterrorism and our preparedness for emerging infections. These issues will be addressed in Atlanta in July 2000 at the Second International Conference on Emerging Infectious Diseases, cosponsored by the CDC, the Council of State and Territorial Epidemiologists, the American Society for Microbiology, the Association of Public Health Laboratories, the World Health Organization, and the National Foundation for CDC.

REFERENCES

The American Medical Association. 1997. *Journal of the American Medical Association,* 278(5).

Armstrong GL, Conn LA, and Pinner RW. 1999. Trends in infectious disease mortality in the United States during the 20th century. *Journal of the American Medical Association,* 281(1):61-66.

Centers for Disease Control and Prevention. 1994. *Addressing Emerging Infectious Disease Threats: A Prevention Strategy for the United States.* Atlanta, Georgia: U.S. Department of Health and Human Services.

——1998. *Preventing Emerging Infectious Diseases: A Strategy for the 21st Century.* Atlanta, Georgia: U.S. Department of Health and Human Services. URL: http//www.cdc.gov.

Clinton W.J. 1999. *Emerging infectious diseases,* 5(4).

——. 1999. Remarks by the President on Keeping America Secure for the 21st Century. National Academy of Sciences, Washington, DC: January 22.

Institute of Medicine, National Research Council. 1999. *Chemical and Biological Terrorism.* Washington, DC: National Academy Press.

Lederberg J, Shope RE, and Oaks Jr., SE, eds. 1992. *Emerging Infections: Microbial Threats to Health in the United States.* Washington, DC: National Academy Press.

Preston R. 1997. *The Cobra Event.* New York, NY: Random House.

Shalala D.E. 1999. Smallpox: setting the research agenda. *Science,* 285:1011.

Torok TJ, Tauxe RV, Wise RP, Livengood JR, Sokolow R, et al. 1997. A large community outbreak of salmonellosis caused by intentional contamination of restaurant salad bars. *Journal of the American Medical Association,* 278(5):389-395.

7. Challenges in Health Technology Development

George M. Milne

While everyone talks about ensuring quality care and focusing on public health, the focus still remains on curbing costs.... But of greater concern is the fact that many of our institutions faced with the day-to-day job of succeeding in today's competitive marketplace are struggling to keep sight of their three-part missions of education, research, and patient care. Our main challenge is to keep our eyes on the goals that we think are important, even as we continue to fight off financial pressures.

—Peter Kohler, M.D.
Chairman, Board of Directors Association of Academic Health Centers

It is ironic that, in terms of science, we live in what may be the most exciting time in history for the health care field. At Pfizer, Inc., strategic thinking is guided by several principles, including, "Don't plunge; don't panic," and, wherever possible, "Experiment your way into the future." We also believe that "innovation is critical to everything we do." These principles apply not only to Pfizer, but also to all of us in health care as we cross the threshold of what may well come to be known as the Century of Biomedicine. We will encounter opportunities to achieve record advances in global health and health care. How effectively we take advantage of these opportunities will depend upon our ability to capitalize upon the changes taking place all around us. It also will depend upon the extent to which we can work synergistically and innovatively with others.

The broad issues and fault lines within health care are global. However, the United States is uniquely positioned to lead the way toward solutions that will effectively serve our institutions, our country, and, most importantly, our patients.

HEALTH CARE: A BOOM MARKET

Today's global health care market is valued at between two and three trillion dollars, and it is growing faster than any other market. There is no reason that health care will not vastly exceed the current fascination with the dot.com marketplace. Both positive and negative factors contribute to this growth. On the plus side are the advances in communication and transportation enabling us to reach the sick and disabled around the world in ways previously impossible. On the negative side is the emergence of drug-resistant bacterial, viral, and fungal infections that are constantly challenging our capacity to find effective therapies.

Perhaps the most dramatic change facing this country today is the growth in the elderly population, a trend with tremendous impact on health care. Health maintenance organizations (HMOs) are facing the challenge of having to provide care for people with more chronic conditions than ever. Pharmaceutical companies are pursuing a greater number of interventions for age-related health problems, such as physical frailty, erectile dysfunction, postmenopausal conditions, and osteoporosis.

The number of older Americans has more than doubled in the last 40 years. In 1960, there were 16.6 million people over age 65 in the United States. In the year 2000, there are 34.7 million—a growth rate of 88 percent, compared to a 34 percent growth rate for those under 65. The U.S.

Census Bureau predicts that by the year 2030, 1 in 5 Americans will be over 65.

The good news is that these Americans will make up the healthiest older generation ever, and that they will want to remain healthy and active. They will insist upon the necessary medical interventions to mitigate the chronic degenerative diseases that heretofore have accompanied old age. This sort of patient demand will fuel more innovative approaches to biomedicine and more efficient methods of delivery.

With easier access to medical information through the media and the Internet, health care consumers are also better educated. Patient advocacy groups have raised awareness about available medicines and therapies and, as a result, expectations have risen regarding the quality of health care that Americans expect to receive. These higher expectations have had a significant impact at the level of national funding. Dr. Florence Haseltine (1999) of the Center for Population Research at the National Institute of Child Health and Human Development recently noted,

> Being an uninformed or silent patient is hazardous to your health. Active patient groups have had a major impact on what is studied, and in fact, in generating the large increase in the National Institutes of Health (NIH) budget,....

Patients are also playing a proactive role in their own health care and, in the past 3 years, the number of people seeking health-related information on the Internet has increased almost eightfold, from 3,000 to over 23 million. In addition, almost twice as many women as men are using the Internet to obtain information on health-related issues, and most of the women are over 50 years of age. These statistics underscore a recent phenomenon: People who need health-related information will find it, and health care professionals have an obligation to provide patients with the accurate information they need to live healthier, better lives.

TECHNOLOGY COMING INTO ITS OWN

Another contributor to the extraordinary opportunity in front of us is the simultaneous coming of age of both information and genomic technology. These companions in innovation are spawning a renaissance in our ability to discover new medicines and identify those patients who are best suited to benefit from them. Currently, all pharmaceutical companies are pursuing various combinations of the same 500 drug targets.

It has been estimated that when the human genome finally is decoded, the number of available targets will increase six- to twentyfold, from 3,000 to 10,000. It is awe-inspiring to consider the enormous capabilities that this discovery will provide for health care practitioners. Patients whose illnesses are now unresponsive to therapies or for whom no effective medicine currently exists will have hope for a better quality of life. We may even find complete cures for diseases that are at present incurable.

As information and genomic technology come of age, other scientific disciplines are maturing into middle age. Diseases such as AIDS and cancer have propelled immunology from its infancy into a sophisticated science. Chemistry has been retooled to allow high-speed analoging and molecular modeling. New biological insights are converting cancer therapies from cytotoxic to cytostatic agents. With the advent of robotics, we can screen more than 50,000 chemical entities in a single week.

Any one of these advances would promote a certain degree of progress. But it is their convergence that has promoted today's dramatic explosion of drug discoveries and development capabilities. An extrapolation from the leaps and bounds afforded by these concomitant advances to the entire field of health care suggests that the future holds unparalleled opportunities. It truly is a remarkable time to be in health care.

Unfortunately, health care is a fragmented enterprise. It is a pastiche of academic institutions, government agencies, the biotechnical field, and big pharmaceutical companies. It is a blend of physicians, nurse practitioners, physician assistants, nurses, pharmacists, and other health care providers. It is a patchwork of HMOs, pharmacy benefit managers, and academic health centers. It involves patients, families, and payers.

People working in pharmaceutical Research and Development (R&D) feel the negative impact of this fragmented focus most acutely. At 7 percent of total health care costs, pharmaceutical R&D offers new and better solutions, but it is seen by many as a prime contributor to the escalating price of good health. If the pharmaceutical field delivers, and patients are effectively treated or illness prevented by novel therapies, patients can enjoy better health at lower cost. This is a tremendous opportunity–but only when viewed broadly across the components of health care delivery. We need to thoughtfully deconstruct the barriers that segregate the various elements of health care delivery. These barriers serve only to separate each of us from the genuine advantages we can achieve if we communicate and collaborate.

GOOD HEALTH IS COST-EFFECTIVE

Health is an ideal we all desire for very personal reasons. But improved health also saves money. Certain diseases are strapping the health care system. Cancer, which afflicts over seven million patients in this country, costs the U.S. health care system more than $100 million per year. Alzheimer's disease costs another $100 million. Almost 19 million people have some form of heart disease, requiring another $116 million. These three diseases, combined with diabetes, arthritis, and stroke, have a combined price tag of one-half billion dollars. Staggering as these figures are, they cannot even begin to measure the personal toll in terms of human suffering.

Innovation presents tremendous opportunities to improve global health. Pfizer is innovating by expanding our Discovery Investments. For instance, in 1999, Pfizer completed the construction of three new laboratory facilities at our sites in Groton, Connecticut; Sandwich, England; and Nagoya, Japan. These buildings will increase our lab space by over a million square feet. It is anticipated that this expansion will enable us to double our discovery output.

Pfizer also continues to build a global health care presence while expanding its understanding of global medical needs. We have thirty clinical R&D sites around the world. To augment internal efforts, we have formed alliances with many external partners in academe and biotechnology. Of course, Pfizer does not have a monopoly on good ideas. To further our own innovation and to promote those of others, Pfizer seeks high-quality partnerships with equally motivated and creative collaborators.

R&D is extremely high-risk, facing significant costs with no guarantee of reward. It takes approximately 12 years from the time a scientist starts developing a new approach to disease treatment for the resulting product to reach the market. Once there, it will enjoy only 12 years of patent exclusivity. Furthermore, reaching the market is the toughest challenge for any new development. Only 1 in 12 treatment candidates survives to reach the market. Today's regulatory environment is increasingly strict: Safety standards are at an all-time high, and the numbers of patients that must be included in clinical trials is climbing steadily. Of those drugs that do reach the market, only 1 in 4 returns a profit on what, by that time, constitutes an extremely high investment. It costs from $250 million to $500 million to bring a single drug through the discovery and development process.

Pfizer has been fortunate; it is at the top of the industry in sales. However, this situation creates enormous expectations from Wall Street and shareholders. Maintaining industry leadership is a challenge in itself. Given the risks, why does Pfizer continue to invest so much in R&D for what may be so little return? By continually developing new treatments, Pfizer demonstrates its belief in the importance of pursuing new opportunities. We also are promoting our partnerships and expanding our global reach through the ways in which we discover, develop, and deliver significant new medicines to the patients who need them. Pfizer can accomplish some of this R&D alone, but we also look to the academic community to partner with us in these efforts.

COLLABORATING WITH ACADEMIC HEALTH CENTERS

One of the most significant roles academic health centers can play for us is providing basic insights into functional genomics. We can and will decipher the human genome, but determining the role genes play in the disease process will be difficult. This is where the academic health center staffs can step in, since these professionals have a historical base of expertise. They have the intellectual capital that is so important to those of us trying to research and develop new medicines. Dr. Kenneth Shaw of Neurogen has defined the situation perfectly:

> What I see as the most daunting challenge facing the industry is how to isolate the subset of potentially useful targets that exist among the thousands that are currently available. No company can do that alone and they turn to academia and the biotech segment of the industry to see what might be important... (Giorgianni, 1999).

Pfizer's core business is the conversion of molecule targets to drugs. We are endeavoring to leverage this status so that in the next 1 to 3 years we can accrue a better understanding of the genome through key academic and biotech alliances while building our own bioinformatics capability. Over the next 1 to 10 years, we hope to establish a network with academic institutions through which we can achieve a better understanding of gene function.

We are also expanding our own internal capabilities in functional genomics. The site of our new discovery technology facility in Cambridge was selected for its proximity to major academic and biotechnical institutions; as a result, we can facilitate better integration of our internal and external R&D efforts. Pfizer has entered into an agreement with four biotechnology companies to enhance high-throughput screening capabilities. Pfizer's Drug Pfinder Program will encourage scientists to identify the chemical entities that will become the medicines of tomorrow. Academic institutions will play an important role in these efforts.

Pfizer also looks to academic health centers to help develop superior clinical measures of disease and disease progression. The genetic revolution of the late 1970s already is generating vast amounts of bioinformation on the pathophysiological basis of diseases. This advance has extended our insights into the disease process and has helped to identify targets for new drugs and other interventions. Unfortunately, the quality and facility of our clinical measures and their link to outcomes have not kept pace.

Numerous biomarkers or new technologies are already in use for their therapeutic benefit or as indicators of disease progression. They include biomarkers for Alzheimer's disease, arthritis, asthma, atherosclerosis, cancer, Huntington's disease, multiple sclerosis, osteoporosis, Parkinson's disease, and stroke.

DISEASE MANAGEMENT: A THREE-LEGGED STOOL

If disease management is viewed as the legs of a stool, one leg would be knowledge of disease mechanisms, the second would be more effective intervention, and the third would be clinical measuring technologies. The last group facilitates early disease detection and precise quantification of disease progression. They also provide the lens through which one can see a disease as it is manifested in individual patients. Is the patient responding? Should the dose be adjusted? Can patients be reassured that there is a benefit to therapy even if no outward signs exist?

Such measures, whether they involve imaging techniques, chemical and immunological tests, or physiological measurements, revolutionize new drug research. They also provide new insights into the disease process itself, leading to a new wave of interventions. The measures are so important to the industry that last year, Pfizer spent in excess of $17 billion funding clinical measures research—research for which it seeks academic partners.

For example, Pfizer has embarked on an ambitious program to discover a variety of noncytotoxic treatments for cancer. Two major strategies involve attacking the unregulated growth of cancer cells and preventing angiogenesis. We have a number of compounds currently in development. Unfortunately, conducting clinical trials is a slow process, especially since we are ethically bound to evaluate drugs only in those patients who are not responding to available therapies.

A new drug about which Pfizer is particularly excited is CP-564,959—a potent and selective inhibitor of the vascular endothelial growth factor (VEGF) receptor, tyrosine kinase.

We know, preclinically, that it can reduce angiogenesis. We are seeking new, noninvasive techniques to determine its efficacy in early clinical trials, but several obvious endpoints include changes in blood volume, blood flow, and vascular permeability. We used a range of imaging techniques to determine whether the drug was having an effect early in the therapeutic process. These techniques included MRI, PET imaging, SPECT imaging, laser Doppler, ultrasonography, and functional CT imaging. Using contrast-enhanced MRIs, we can see the mammary carcinoma. After treatment with an anti-VEGF monoclonal antibody, we were able to demonstrate that vascular permeability was reduced within 24 hours. This technique was validated by demonstrating a high degree of correlation with histopathologic endpoints. We are also pursuing other means to fine—tune our clinical trials.

Pfizer has joined with nine other pharmaceutical companies and also with five genome centers (Cold Spring Harbor, Sanger Center, Stanford Human Genome Center, Washington University School of Medicine, and

Whitehead Institute) in the Single Nucleotide Polymorphism (SNP) Consortium. The goals include decoding the human genome within the next 2 years and identifying genetic markers of disease.

Discovering these markers may enable pharmaceutical companies like Pfizer to enroll patients who will most likely benefit from a particular therapeutic approach. It will also help us identify patients who are at risk for developing a particular disease. The SNP Consortium also may identify genetic-level differences that account for the incidence of disease, thus enabling us to pursue even more relevant therapies.

MANAGING DISEASE, CONTROLLING COSTS

Health care professionals also are called upon to innovate superior outcomes in health care management. Effective pharmaceutical interventions have had documented success in reducing overall health care costs. For example, glucose-lowering agents have averted expenditures of $1.2 billion to $1.6 billion in disability among diabetes patients. Anticancer drugs have restored $1 billion in the lifetime earnings of cancer patients. Antipsychotic drugs save an estimated $148 billion in direct and indirect costs annually, and lithium treatment for manic-depression has saved approximately $7 billion. This is only a sampling of effective therapies that benefit the patient and the health care system and the health care system of a nation.

HMOs increasingly recognize the benefit of disease management. More than one-half are managing asthma and diabetes, but the percentage declines precipitously in relation to congestive heart failure, breast cancer, depression, hypercholesterolemia, HIV/AIDS, high blood pressure, peptic ulcer, prostate cancer, osteoporosis, allergic rhinitis, and arthritis (in that order).

Another example of shortsightedness is a recent study of elderly schizophrenic patients. When New Hampshire restricted the number of prescriptions being reimbursed by Medicaid, the elderly entered nursing homes at a 60 percent greater rate. In other words, when drug utilization fell by 35 percent, nursing home admissions rose by 60 percent. Thus, while the reimbursement caps saved an average of $57 per year on drugs, additional costs rose by $1,530.36, accrued through increased visits to mental health clinics and emergency rooms (Somerai et al., 1994).

Patient noncompliance is also a serious problem. According to the Wilkerson Group's recent estimate, only one-half of all patients requiring chronic care follow their physician's instructions concerning medication. The National Pharmaceutical Council estimates that patient noncompliance costs the health care system more than $100 billion each year in increased hospital and nursing home admissions, lost productivity, and premature deaths (PhRMA, 1998).

What is the answer to spiraling health care costs? We believe it to be a combination of innovative solutions to the above-mentioned health care dilemmas, coupled with effective therapy. Such a combination also could help patients live longer and healthier lives.

Programs such as Pfizer Health Solutions (PHS) are providing health care organizations with innovative, technology-based clinical solutions as well as business resources. Using Web-based technology, we are seeking to integrate data sets; the goal is to reduce the pervasive redundancy that encumbers health care. The resulting increase in efficiency will benefit all.

Technology is affecting medical resources in other ways. Handwritten records (and the resulting need for transcriptions) are being replaced by electronic medical records. Soon a patient's entire medical history will be available instantaneously, dramatically expediting the process of diagnosis and treatment. In addition, electronic records will reduce medical transcription costs by an estimated 60 to 80 percent.

Electronic medical records will significantly enhance data capture and communication. We will be able to perform instantaneous outcomes research. Is the patient responding? Would another medicine be more effective? Information technology also will allow us to examine large numbers of individuals to determine who is at greatest risk for particular illnesses and who may require more proactive or aggressive therapy. This, too, will alleviate costs.

To take advantage of the opportunities opening up to us through advances in information technology, we will need to engage in thoughtful clinical research and develop a broadly integrated and patient-centered health care delivery system. Breaking down traditional barriers is a challenging task, but one that academic health centers are uniquely qualified to handle. As wellsprings of innovation in health care, they are an ideal environment in which to test out these new methods.

HMOs traditionally have been engaged in acute disease intervention. Gradually, this emphasis is shifting, with people living longer and developing more chronic conditions, and with data indicating that whole body health saves money in the long run. PHS and similar programs are giving HMOs the technology to monitor an individual's entire health history, while implementing dietary modification, stress reduction, and smoking cessation programs. Health care is not just about treating a specific disease any more.

THE TRACHOMA PROGRAM: A GLOBAL DELIVERY SUCCESS STORY

One of Pfizer's recent innovative international programs demonstrates the challenge of global health care delivery in developing nations, and also the value of partnerships. In 1998, with the support of the World Health Organization, Pfizer and the Edna McConnell Clark Foundation launched the International Trachoma Initiative to provide a comprehensive prevention and treatment program in countries where the disease is endemic.

Trachoma, caused by chlamydia trachoma bacteria, is the leading cause of preventable blindness in the world. Approximately six million people are blind as a result of this condition, and more than another 146 million are actively infected. Trachoma incidence is directly related to socioeconomic development. Not surprisingly, trachoma is most prevalent in parts of Africa, Asia, Australia, and Central and South America.

Based on early research, Pfizer's oral antibiotic, Zithromax, appeared to be particularly effective in treating this condition. The traditional therapy, topical tetracycline, is effective, but compliance is poor and reinfection rates are high. In contrast, Zithromax is administered in a single 1-gram dose, which works for several weeks. Thus, infected individuals need only one treatment—an important consideration when treating patients in highly remote and poverty-stricken locations.

The International Trachoma Initiative is being conducted in five countries and to date has achieved striking results. In Morocco, trachoma prevalence has been reduced by 40 percent through a comprehensive strategy of surgery, antibiotics, face-washing, and environmental change known as SAFE. However, the success of this initiative called for more than having enough money and providing the right drug. It necessitated developing strong partnerships with local health officials and building a health care infrastructure that makes effective health care delivery possible. It also required engaging each country's political will to eliminate blindness within a set timeframe. Sadly, this essential combination of factors is not present in all countries affected by trachoma, which poses a major challenge to those of us who seek to improve global health.

Numerous diseases around the world today are going unchecked by adequate treatment, and many people suffer from them. Trachoma is just one small success story in a world crying for more. Pfizer is committed to finding solutions to these challenges by recognizing and taking advantage of the many opportunities that surround us. The future holds unparalleled opportunities for those of us in health care. By working together, we can make significant strides in helping people live longer, healthier lives around the world.

REFERENCES

Giorgianni. 1999. Perspective on health care and medical research. *The Pfizer Journal,* 3(2):27.

Haseltine, Florence. 1999. Perspective on health care and biomedical research, *The Pfizer Journal,* 3(2):31.

Kohler P. 1999. In *AHC Annual Report 1999.* Washington, DC: Association of Academic Health Centers.

PhRMA (Pharmaceutical Research and Manufacturers of America). 1998. *Industry Profile.* Washington: PhRMA.

Somerai SB, McLaughlin TJ, Ross-Degnan D, Casteris CS, and Bollini P. 1994. Effects of limiting Medicaid drug-reimbursement benefits on the use of psychotropic agents and acute mental health services by patients with schizophrenia. *New England Journal of Medicine,* 331(10):650.

8. Global Tools for Technology Assessment

JOEL J. NOBEL

TECHNOLOGY ASSESSMENT, THE FOCUS OF THIS paper, is one of many technology-related programs available today. Before we consider this topic, it is important to note that the current academic research environment suffers from two significant weaknesses. These are (1) the need to rely upon financing, and (2) an intransigent adherence to the ideal of academic freedom. These weaknesses have both stimulated and confounded the development of technology assessment.

Before examining the tools for technology assessment, however, it is helpful to look at a catalog of research centers such as *Healthcare Standards Directory** published annually by ECRI. It contains the intellectual substrata upon which technology assessment is built.

ECRI is not an academic institution, although it has educated more than 600 individuals from forty nations over the past 15 years. Numerous fundamental differences exist between ECRI and the institutions affiliated

*ECRI. 1999. *Health Care Standards Directory.* Plymouth Meeting, PA: ECRI.

with the Association of Academic Health Centers (AHC) from the perspective of organizational philosophy, methods, and values.

ECRI is a 32-year-old, nonprofit, 501(c)(3) health services research organization, located on its own 12-acre campus in a suburb of Philadelphia. It has a full-time, interdisciplinary staff of about 250, including physicians, basic medical scientists, engineers, attorneys, information specialists, software developers, and health care planners. We have branch offices in the United Kingdom, Malaysia, and Abu Dhabi, as well as affiliates in South Africa, Brazil, and Australia. ECRI is a collaborating center of the World Health Organization. We focus on all aspects of health care technology, health care risk management, quality assurance, and health care environmental management.

DEFINING HEALTH TECHNOLOGY AND ASSESSMENT

The terms "health care technology" and "health care technology assessment" have different meanings to different constituencies in different parts of the world. The definition of "health care technology" employed in academe and in governments worldwide, as originated by the now-defunct U.S. Congressional Office of Technology Assessment, encompasses pharmaceuticals, biotechnologies, devices, equipment, and medical and surgical procedures. By contrast, the U.S. bioengineering community has the more narrow view that health care technology is synonymous with equipment. Many device manufacturers see it the same way.

"Health care technology assessment" is generally understood to mean an objective evaluation (based upon solid evidence) of the safety, efficacy, and clinical- and cost-effectiveness of a health care technology. This evaluation is conducted either in isolation or in comparison to competing technologies that are intended to meet the same diagnostic, therapeutic, or supportive goals. For some technology assessments, ethical and legal examination also may be significant.

From a biomedical device manufacturer's perspective, technology assessment is a potential barrier to market acceptance and also may be a roadblock to obtaining regulatory authorization to market a product. From a pharmaceutical manufacturer's point of view, technology assessment carries the added burden and discipline of pharmacoeconomics. From a clinical engineer's perspective, technology assessment often is just a sophisticated term for the prepurchase evaluation and economic feasibility analyses that are conducted on equipment under consideration by a clinical institution.

Our organization operates with the broadest definitions of technology and assessment as they are employed in the fields of academe and government. Nonetheless, ECRI has programs that are encompassed by any of the above definitions.

Why does technology assessment even exist as an intellectual discipline, given the extraordinary history of high-quality clinical research that has been undertaken by our many academic medical institutions—research that has been published, after exhaustive peer review, in our esteemed journals?

The reason that technology assessment, pharmacoeconomics, outcomes research, and similar fields even exist is that these glowing assertions about the academic peer-review research model are, quite frankly, inaccurate. Most peer-review journal articles emerging from academic health centers today simply will not support evidence-based medicine. Most follow the classical pattern of descriptive or experimental science, sometimes with a statistical veneer. Others are narrow and lack context. They are of unacceptable quality to support serious decision making about what works, how well it works, and whether or not a particular therapy is worth implementing. The proof of my assertion lies in the following observations.

CAN PEER-REVIEW JOURNALS WITHSTAND SCRUTINY?

The first step in technology assessment is to collect information about everything that is known regarding a diagnostic or therapeutic method or product, and to examine the related study and statistical design of the journal articles. Unfortunately, when examined in this context, the score is dismal. Typically, fewer than 5 percent of peer-reviewed journal articles in oncology or surgery can withstand serious scrutiny, nor do they stand up well over the years. It is only a little better for the cardiovascular literature.

The clinical research literature is inadequate for a number of reasons:

1. F*inancial, psychological, career, or ego incentives bias the research process.*

Caring about results distorts a researcher's thinking, and inhibits his or her capacity to hear criticism. So does the motive to publish.

2. *Responsibility for clinical research is too diffuse.* It may include the granting agency and grant reviewers, the applying individuals, the Institutional Review Board (IRB), the academic department and its hierarchy, the academic institution, the research team members, and, of course, the principal investigators, journal editor, and peer reviewers. This collective process, while it may be of significant value for many reasons, also effectively dilutes responsibility.

According to the journals, the principal investigators are the responsible parties. According to the institutions, it is the journal review process itself and the involved departments that are responsible. The institutions neglect to recall that a university is a corporation, and as such, it is responsible for the work of its employees. The question is: Are the researchers indeed university employees, or is the university just a fiduciary and conduit for Federal funds?

3. *Research in academic centers is not managed.* Quality guidelines are virtually unknown, let alone enforced. An academic corporation produces intellectual products rather than physical ones, but it lacks the analog of a quality control manager that we would find, for instance, in a can opener factory. The can opener corporation will not survive long if it produces a poor product. Academic corporations, on the other hand, routinely blame others and get away with it.

ECRI's 1991 survey of 143 medical schools in the United States and Canada showed that none had research quality guidelines that were as good as a drug company is required to have by the Food and Drug Administration (FDA). Their guidelines are not even as rigorous as those required by the Federal Trade Commission (FTC) for an advertising agency. None of the medical schools' guidelines contained such basic elements as retention time for research records, control of laboratory notebooks, backup requirements for computer data, standards for data auditing, or any of the core quality measures that are found in almost all other institutions conducting research or producing goods.

FINANCES AND FREEDOM: THE ROOTS OF DISTORTED RESEARCH

The two most critical factors contributing to the distortion of medical research today are its financial context and how the concept of academic freedom plays out in the research component of a university.

Research funding sources, funding relationships, and the hope or promise of future money distort motivation, method, thought processes, results, and the presentation of information. Because medical researchers consider themselves to be honest scientists doing noble work, they seem to believe they effectively cleanse money by taking it from unclean sources and using it for altruistic purposes. (Perhaps this perception has its roots in the modern university's early origin in the church and monastery.)

Academics insist that the value of academic freedom, in and of itself, should take precedence over any type of institutional oversight or responsibility for the quality of research. This is a deeply entrenched belief, complete with all the baggage that goes with holding onto such a value system.

Consider, as well, science's basic form and method: One's theory must be proven. Unfortunately, belief in a theory is often more powerful than the evidence itself. This belief sometimes distorts the methods chosen to demonstrate the evidence. There is a subtle connection between theoretical belief, with its nearly religious intensity, and the way that belief distorts the quality of science, including clinical research. It all comes back to belief, after all: Consider that both religion and medical research are focused on life, death, and salvation—for both patients and scientists. In practice, at least, science is synonymous with emotion and mystical belief.

There is a frequent disconnect between the researchers' objectives and genuine national and social priorities. For instance, Medicare just held the first meeting of its new Coverage Advisory Committee. The topic was whether high-dose chemotherapy with autologous bone marrow transplant or stem-cell transplant benefits patients with multiple myeloma more than standard chemotherapy does. The committee was supposed to draw on evidence-based medicine, but not a single randomized, controlled trial comparing these clinical strategies has been completed in the United States. Medicare spends $700 million a day on this disease, yet our medical research institutions are not producing the evidence base to support this vital program that serves 40 million people.

Systematic and continuing assessment programs are undertaken or supported by numerous government agencies around the world, a limited number of academic institutions, several specialized nonprofit institutes such as ECRI, and a few commercial organizations. Most of these organizations are located in the United States, Canada, and Northern Europe. The earliest efforts to assess technology began in the 1960s at the U.S. Congressional Office of Technology Assessment. They were intended to provide data to underpin wise social investments in health care as well as other arenas. For example, ECRI's program was first funded by a W.K. Kellogg Foundation grant in 1982. Shortly thereafter, ECRI commenced an academic program at the University of Houston Medical School.

THE IDEAL OF INTERNATIONAL ASSESSMENT

In the early to mid 1980s, a group of academics came together to put forward the inevitable concept of an international organization to promote technology assessment. That concept evolved into what is now the 16-year-old International Society for Technology Assessment in Health Care (ISTAHC). ISTAHC has over 1,000 members, and ECRI will be privileged to host its annual meeting in Philadelphia in June 2001.

In addition, within ISTAHC, there are special-interest groups, such as those for developing countries whose needs in technology assessment are different from those of industrialized nations. Beyond ISTAHC, a number of other organizations are now actively promoting technology assessment. The International Association for Health Technology Assessment (INAHTA) is an international organization of government and nonprofit technology assessment groups. The International Society for Pharmacoeconomics, which has approximately 1,000 members, has a heavy concentration of members from both pharmaceutical companies and academic organizations.

Technology assessment is closely connected to regulatory decisions that permit the marketing of a new diagnostic or therapeutic modality. It is even more closely connected to reimbursement decisions. The Health Care

Financing Administration (HCFA) has increasingly depended on technology assessment to undergird its coverage decisions for Medicare, as have many private insurers and HMOs. One should not imagine, however, that the rational processes of technology assessment and its logical conclusions necessarily carry the day. Health care itself is a highly politicized framework for decision making, especially in this country. A case history later in this paper will demonstrate the intellectual, financial, clinical, emotional, and political aspects of such decision making. Technology assessment seems to have a greater impact in Canada, Sweden, and France.

In the United States, the leading Federal agency for health care technology assessment is the Department of Health and Human Services' Agency for Healthcare Research and Quality (AHRQ), formerly the Agency for Health Care Policy and Research. It has working relationships with other government agencies, such as FDA and HCFA, and has taken the initiative in coordinating and funding some of the most significant technology assessments undertaken in the United States. AHRQ no longer conducts major assessments in-house. It has designated twelve institutions as Evidence-Based Practice Centers, to which it contracts for specific studies. Among them are Johns Hopkins University, McMaster University, Stanford University, the University of North Carolina at Chapel Hill, Duke University, and ECRI. ECRI, however, also has its own self-funded program, which is larger than its AHRQ-funded program; this is funded by sales of its reports to the members of what is, in effect, an international cooperative. ECRI has been undertaking technology assessments intensively for the past decade.

Most academic and governmental technology assessment programs have arisen at an existing institution within a health policy framework. Some of these technology assessment programs operate within quasigovernmental organizations. In this country, nongovernmental programs typically have arisen in a university health policy context, sometimes within a medical school itself and sometimes within a medical school in association with the university's business or law school. In the private sector, technology assessment programs have arisen and sometimes broken away from their parent corporations, such as Blue Cross, Battelle, and RAND.

AN AUTONOMOUS ASSESSMENT PROGRAM

The ECRI technology assessment program is unique, in that it evolved naturally within an autonomous, nonprofit institute with strong bioengineering antecedents and a traditional program of medical product evaluation. Essentially, we evolved very much the way Consumer Reports did with its evaluations of cars and appliances. That tradition has included very tough conflict-of-interest rules, which would be dysfunctional, not to mention impossible to implement, within an academic environment. Our engineering antecedents have endowed our technology assessment program with a different type of technical competence, an insistence on precision, a truly interdisciplinary workforce, and a strong international reputation for integrity.

For the past three decades, ECRI's conflict-of-interest rules have been the hallmark of the organization. We accept no grants, gifts, contracts, or other financial support from medical device or pharmaceutical manufacturers or distributors. ECRI employees are not permitted to own stock in or independently consult for such organizations, and every employee's IRS returns, from janitor to chief executive officer, are audited prior to filing to be sure that every individual in ECRI's employ is behaving, individually, the way we behave as an organization.

No organization has tougher conflict-of-interest rules. Why is this important for product evaluation and technology assessment? ECRI wishes to avoid the appearance, as well as any possibility, of inappropriate influence bearing on our studies. However, financial distortion of intellectual results is only one possible source of bias. Two others are emotion and ego, and for these we have several very specific safeguards distinctly different from those found in the classical academic research peer-review model. These very intensive methods, which have withstood the test of time, include independent auditing of laboratory notebooks and calculations, comprehensive internal reviews, extensive outside reviews of ECRI's work before dissemination, and an external audit committee that independently examines both the work processes and the results of our technology assessment program. This audit committee has prerogatives, and teeth. We have diminished the impact of ego by eliminating the concept of authorship. ECRI's ideas and publications are institutional and not attributed to individuals. ECRI authors are never identified. In short, ECRI's intellectual and publishing model is far more exacting and intensive than the academic peer-reviewed journal.

Most technology assessment studies carried out by the types of institutions mentioned above are essentially examinations of the existing knowledge base as expressed in the clinical and peer-reviewed journal literature and the gray literature. As previously noted, the peer-review literature leaves much to be desired. The gray literature, which may include studies undertaken by manufacturers or individual hospitals or public agencies, is often more useful in technology assessment than is the peer-reviewed journal literature. It may be more focused, better documented, and more timely. However, sometimes it, too, is virtually useless.

The concept of peer review is not limited to formal journals. What lies behind this assertion? When ECRI undertakes a technology assessment, one of the first tasks is to determine what is known about a subject. We launch extensive literature searches, employing choices from almost 200 different databases. Some are, indeed, general databases of articles from peer-reviewed journals such as MEDLINE and EMBASE. Others are very specialized and contain much valued data that are never published in journal articles. One database and resource is ECRI's own extensive International Health Technology Assessment database, which we have been compiling over the last 7 years, partly under contract with the National Library of Medicine. Our internal databases are even more comprehensive. Two other international databases that are important for technology assessment are those of the Cochrane Collaboration and DARE at the University of York, both of which are based in the United Kingdom.

Each of ECRI's technology assessments typically examines several thousand documents comprising the evidence, primarily the clinical research literature. Our reports can be several hundred pages long. We do not publish our findings in the peer-reviewed literature. Nonetheless, our own assessments are extensively peer-reviewed. So are the many assessments and clinical trial reports published as monographs by other organizations, including scores of government technology assessment organizations. ECRI's annual *Healthcare Standards Directory* provides a detailed list of organizations worldwide that produce health technology assessments, as well as the assessments each organization has produced.

ABMT/HDC: UNSOUND RESEARCH, TRAGIC RESULTS

To illustrate the unusual challenges associated with technology assessment, the case history of autologous bone marrow transplantation with high-dose chemotherapy (ABMT/HDC) for metastatic breast cancer works well because it illustrates virtually everything that can go wrong when money and ego distort clinical chores and research.

The underlying principle for this therapy is conceptually simple. If a moderate amount of chemotherapy cures some cancer, then more intensive chemotherapy in higher doses will cure more cancers. Of course, the problem with high-dose chemotherapy is that it also kills blood-forming elements. Thus, the concept arose of removing bone marrow or stem cells from the patient, administering chemotherapy at approximately ten times the normal dose, isolating the patient to prevent infection, and then reinserting blood-forming elements.

This clinical procedure was used in a variety of academic health centers throughout the United States; yet, for the first 17 years, not a single randomized, controlled trial was undertaken or reported. Furthermore, the clinical trial reports that made this therapy appear successful simply ignored the phenomenon of early deaths. Procedure-related mortality was 10 percent to 20 percent within the first 30 days, but this was excluded from the reported results. When ECRI first examined this technology in 1993, we were appalled. We started by pulling approximately 3,600 peer-reviewed journal articles in the clinical literature and closely examined 800 of them. Ultimately, we narrowed them down to fifty-five useful articles. Most studies were poorly designed and simply unacceptable. We then undertook a series of highly complex, quantitative analyses of the available but limited data, and concluded that this procedure, based on all the available evidence, had four nasty characteristics:

1. On average, the therapy failed to extend life when compared to conventional chemotherapy.
2. The bone marrow transplant procedure itself killed about 15 percent

of the patients receiving it within the first 30 days.

3. The procedure costs $100,000 to $200,000. We suspected that, where there is money, business and commercial physicians would not be far behind. Sure enough, these entities already had started a clinical service franchise to provide high-dose chemotherapy with autologous stem cell replacement. Response Technologies (chartered in the Cayman Islands and privately owned) lobbied for reimbursement.
4. The procedure was so rigorous that it severely punished patients and their families: It traditionally required inpatient isolation precautions for 30 days, effectively disconnecting patients from their normal family environments at a time of great fear and stress in their lives.

In short, we found that ABMT/HDC therapy is atrocious and exploitive medicine. It was no great surprise that some oncologists agreed with ECRI while some attacked us. Several physicians suggested that we obtain additional data from the North American Bone Marrow Transplant Registry to which many of them had been contributing data. We paid the registry some $5,000 to extract specific data for us, incorporated it into a second study—and concluded that the situation was even worse than we originally reported.

Remarkably enough, the day before we were due to publish our report, the registry withdrew permission for us to use their data. We believe that they did this simply because the clinicians who were contributing data to the registry did not like our conclusions. By this time, however, the registry's permission no longer mattered. We had addressed the problem from so many different perspectives that the conclusion was inescapable.

In the meantime, the political and social environment for ABMT/HDC therapy itself had become intense. The public paradigm was "dying women, greedy insurance companies, and legislative saviors." Federal and state legislatures became involved. Some legislators became intensely involved with the issues because they had family members with breast cancer. Some jurisdictions required that insurance companies cover this therapy, while others, based on our data, did not. Once again, some oncologists thought we were right, and others were outraged.

One academic oncologist who was a particularly passionate advocate of this therapy openly condemned our study. However, he had never even read the study and indicated that he did not need to do so because it could not possibly be right. In the meantime, it became increasingly difficult to enroll women in randomized studies. Nobody wanted the standard treatment. The next step was to meet with the National Breast Cancer Coalition to seek its review of ECRI's study. The National Breast Cancer Coalition is not composed of fanatical advocates; it has excellent scientific capability. It supported our study, then produced a 60-page version of our 250-page study in lay language for breast cancer patients. It did not tell patients what to do. It simply gave them the facts so they could make up their own minds. (ECRI has published this brochure on its Web site.)

Meanwhile, the National Cancer Institute (NCI) was funding several randomized, controlled trials. The upshot of the entire sorry episode is that in the spring of 1999, after conducting these trials, NCI came to the same conclusion that ECRI had come to 5 years earlier, although they expressed it somewhat more obliquely in order to avoid offending the advocates of the therapy.

During those 5 years between ECRI's report and NCI's similar conclusions, literally thousands of patients died prematurely. Using a very conservative estimate of a 10 percent procedure-induced mortality rate (arguably now down to 3 percent or less in certain centers), ABMT/HDC therapy killed approximately 2,000 to 3,000 patients. The oncologists in the academic research community who passionately advocated this procedure to the point of ignoring alternative views should be ashamed of themselves. Sadly, some practitioners still cling to their belief in ABMT/HDC therapy, regardless of all the evidence against it.

The obvious question is, how did a relatively obscure, small, nonacademic organization get it right when almost everybody else got it wrong? The answer is simple: ECRI did not care about the results. We had no bias toward positive or negative results because the outcome did not affect our purse. We do not provide clinical services, so the results of the study had no effect on our reputation. There were no individual egos involved.

OBJECTIVITY = ACCURACY

Herein lies the key lesson for technology assessment and any other research: Without objectivity, research is useless. Objectivity demands certain preconditions related to conflict of interest. Even more important, objectivity demands that egotists and fools within the medical research community should not be permitted to suppress data and distort information simply because they do not like the facts or stand to lose money if they are revealed.

It is helpful to recall that the modern university emerged from monasteries and schools of theology. The term professor, now understood to mean a highly educated, intellectually competent, and wise individual, comes from the original, simple meaning: "to profess faith in the ordained religious beliefs and authority." Let us not forget that faith-based clinical research does not lead to evidence-based medicine.

9. *Global Issues in Clinical Trials*

ROBERT J. LEVINE

IN THE 1990s, THE INTEREST IN CONDUCTING MULTI-national clinical trials increased dramatically, sparked in great part by the AIDS pandemic. This situation, in turn, raised an urgent need to treat patients already infected with HIV and reduce the incidence of new infections. As a result, sponsors and investigators from industrialized countries are now supporting a majority of the AIDS-related clinical trials being conducted in the resource-poor countries of the world where the need is most acute. The inhabitants of these countries are, in effect, serving as research subjects.

This situation is highly problematic since research involving human subjects must be conducted in compliance with existing legal and ethical standards. However, the recent rise in multinational collaborations has forced us to recognize that standards for trials in industrialized nations may not be readily applicable to trials conducted in less-developed countries.

What is needed is an international code of ethics that would be applicable to all regions of the world. Efforts in this area have led to a growing recognition that the documents on which we currently rely when evaluating human research have serious flaws that limit their applicability not only in the Third World, but also in the countries where they were developed.

It has been said that the AIDS pandemic presents us with novel ethical problems that necessitate revisions of the current ethical codes and regulations. This is not entirely true. The reputedly novel problems presented by AIDS were there all along. The specific social and political features of the AIDS pandemic merely forced us to attend to problems that should have been addressed long ago (Levine, 1994).

Since World War II, three major international codes of research ethics have been developed: The Nuremberg Code, the World Medical Association's Declaration of Helsinki, and the International Ethical Guidelines for Biomedical Research Involving Human Subjects of the Council of International Organizations of Medical Sciences (CIOMS and WHO, 1993). A more complete discussion of these documents and their relation to each other appear in the author's paper on this topic (Levine, 1996). The current article concentrates on the Declaration of Helsinki because most critics of multinational clinical trials base their criticisms on interpretations of this document.

THE DECLARATION OF HELSINKI: OVERDUE FOR CHANGE

The Declaration of Helsinki was first promulgated by the World Medical Association at its meeting in Helsinki in 1964. It has been amended several times. The Declaration urgently needs revision for two important reasons (Levine, 1999).

First, the reasoning is frequently illogical. For example, the Declaration categorizes all research as either therapeutic or nontherapeutic. Such categorization is fallacious, and documents that rely on such oversimplication necessarily contain errors. These errors, though not so intended by their authors, are a source of great embarrassment when exposed.

Second, the document is seriously out of touch with contemporary ethical thinking. For example, it takes an unnecessarily rigid stance against placebo-controlled clinical trials. Because of this error and others, the Declaration is widely disregarded. As a result, investigators in every academic health center in the United States routinely conduct research that violates the Declaration's standards. Such widespread and routine disregard undermines the Declaration's authority and credibility.

Let us examine the distinction between therapeutic guidelines set forth in Section II of the Declaration and nontherapeutic research in Section III. Putting one article from Section II in immediate proximity to another from Section III elucidates the flaw in logic:

> II.6 The doctor can combine medical research with professional care . . . only to the extent that . . . research is justified by its potential diagnostic or therapeutic value for the patient.
>
> III.2 The subjects should be volunteers—either healthy persons or patients for whom the experimental design is not related to the patient's illness.

Consider what is ruled out by this pair of articles, namely, all research in the fields of pathogenesis, pathophysiology, and epidemiology. For example, a nontherapeutic study examining the role of neurotransmitters in the pathogenesis of mental depression could not be justified in terms of its potential diagnostic or therapeutic benefit to the patient. Therefore, according to the Declaration, it could only be conducted on normal volunteers or on patients who have some disease other than depression. This sort of absurdity reveals that the Declaration is both illogical and embarrassing.

The concept of therapeutic research is equally troubling. When all of the components of a given research protocol are nontherapeutic, use of the term "nontherapeutic research" might be justified. However, every clinical trial contains some components that are nontherapeutic. If we evaluate entire protocols as either therapeutic or nontherapeutic, as required by the Declaration of Helsinki, we end up with what I call "the fallacy of the package deal." Those who use this distinction typically classify as therapeutic research any protocol that includes one or more component intended to be therapeutic; therefore, the nontherapeutic components of the protocol are justified improperly according to the more permissive standards developed for therapeutic research.

Such erroneous justifications in the recent past include the following situations:

- In trials of thrombolytic therapy, repeated coronary angiograms were conducted upon patients who had clinical indications for only one.

- Liver biopsies were performed for no reason other than to disguise treatment assignments in a double-blind, placebo-controlled trial.
- Repeated endoscopies were performed in a population of patients with peptic ulcers who had clinical indications for no more than one.
- A placebo was administered by way of a catheter inserted in the coronary artery.

None of the above procedures was unethical. However, they should not be justified according to standards developed for therapeutic research. These examples illustrate the necessity of using a vocabulary that enables us to evaluate these research components accurately. In the 1970s, the United States and Canada, each recognizing the problems caused by the distinction between therapeutic and nontherapeutic research, purged these concepts from their regulations and guidelines. In the United States, in response to recommendations made by the National Commission for the Protection of Human Subjects of Biomedical and Behavioral Research (1979), Federal regulations were revised in the early 1980s to classify interventions and procedures, and not entire protocols, as either beneficial or nonbeneficial (Levine, 1979, 1988).

In the language of the regulations for research involving children, interventions or procedures are classified as either those that hold out the prospect of direct benefit or those that do not hold out such a prospect. They are referred to in the regulations as either beneficial or nonbeneficial. The justification of beneficial procedures is similar in principle to that employed in the practice of medicine: The intervention or procedure must offer some prospect of improved health for the individual patient-subject. Moreover, in most cases, the therapeutic procedure being researched should be used only if no other superior therapeutic procedures are known to exist. There is no ceiling imposed on the degree of risk that may be imposed in the pursuit of therapeutic benefit—only that it must be reasonable in relation to the anticipated benefits.

Obviously, nontherapeutic procedures cannot be justified in terms of their expected benefit for the patient-subject. They must be justified instead by the benefits one hopes to produce for society. The amount of risk that may be presented to vulnerable subjects by nonbeneficial procedures is limited by the regulations' so-called threshold standards. For example, for research involving children, only those nonbeneficial interventions or procedures that present no more than minimal risk may be employed without special justification.

Interventions and procedures that involve children and that present only a minor increase over minimal risk must be justified on the grounds that the procedure itself "is likely to yield . . . knowledge . . . which is of vital importance for the understanding or amelioration of the subjects' disorder or condition." Furthermore, the regulation requires that "the intervention or procedure presents experiences to subjects that are reasonably commensurate with those inherent in [the subjects'] actual or expected medical . . . situations, . . . (45 CFR §46.406). Interventions or procedures that present more than a minor increase over minimal risk must be reviewed and approved at the national level.

MODERN ETHICS AND THE THERAPEUTIC METHOD

The Declaration of Helsinki not only has logical flaws; it also is out of touch with contemporary ethical thinking as is illustrated in the Declaration's Article II.3:

> II.3 In any medical study, every patient—including those in a control group, if any—should be assured that the best proven diagnostic and therapeutic method is being employed. This does not exclude the use of inert placebo in studies where no proven diagnostic or therapeutic method exists.

This article rules out the development of new therapies for conditions for which there are already existing "proven" therapies. One could not evaluate a new therapy without withholding those that have already been demonstrated to be safe and effective for the same indication. Strict application of this standard would have prevented the evaluation of the efficacy of cimetidine and other H2 receptor antagonists for the treatment of peptic ulcer purely because the withholding of belladonna and its derivatives would have been considered an unethical withholding of the "best proven therapeutic method." Similarly, the development of new and improved antihypertensive drugs would have ceased with the establishment of the ganglionic blockers.

Article II.3 also forbids placebo controls in clinical trials where withholding a proven therapy poses virtually no risk. Consider research in the field of analgesics and antihistamines. No experienced person would ever recommend that researchers be required to have an active control in the evaluation of a new analgesic. Article II.3 also rules out the use of placebo controls in clinical trials, such as trials of new antihypertensives or of new oral hypoglycemic agents, in which there is a very remote possibility of an adverse consequence as a result of withholding the active drug. Insisting on active controls in these areas would introduce major inefficiencies into the research enterprise with very little compensating benefit. The amount of injury to research subjects that would be prevented by requiring active controls is so small that it can be, and generally is, considered negligible.

Placebo-controlled trials of analgesics, antihypertensives, and oral hypoglycemics are conducted often, and the results are published in medical journals. Parenthetically, it is worth noting that the publication of such studies is yet another routine violation of the Declaration of Helsinki. Article I.8 holds, "Reports of experimentation not in accordance with the principles laid down in this Declaration should not be accepted for publication."

BEST PROVEN METHOD: ETHICS OR IMPERIALISM?

The most controversial interpretation of the Declaration's Article II.3 requires the provision of the best proven therapeutic method available in the industrialized countries be provided, even when conducting research in countries in which such therapy is not available.

This interpretation has provoked the most acrimonious debate in the field of research ethics since the 1970s.

The debate began when *The New England Journal of Medicine* published an article that denounced as unethical the clinical trials being carried out in certain developing countries to evaluate the effectiveness of the short-duration regimen of AZT in preventing perinatal transmission of HIV infection (Lurie and Wolfe, 1997). The editor of *The New England Journal* opined that these trials were, in certain respects, reminiscent of the notorious Tuskegee Syphilis Studies (Angell, 1997). In contemporary American culture, this is a powerful metaphor for evil in the field of research ethics. The other side of the controversy is exemplified by a statement made by a physician-researcher from Uganda, one of the countries in which the trials were being conducted. He accused the editor of a form of "ethical imperialism" that asserts that the Western vision of research ethics must dominate the conduct of research everywhere in the world.

Let us consider the above AZT clinical trial as a case study. At the time the trial began, and indeed to this day, the standard in industrialized countries such as the United States is the so-called 076 regimen. The name comes from the AIDS Clinical Trial Group (ACTG) protocol number 76, which established its safety and efficacy. The 076 regimen reduces perinatal transmission of HIV infection by about 67 percent. In 1997, the cost of the chemicals alone for treating each infected pregnant woman was approximately US$800.

Why can we not simply provide the 076 regimen to women infected with HIV in developing countries? First and foremost, the cost would be prohibitive. In many of the sub-Saharan African countries in which these trials were being carried out, $800 per woman is approximately 80 times the annual per capita health expenditure. But the cost of the chemicals is not the only problem. What follows is a brief review of some of the other problems. For a more complete examination of this topic, see Levine (1998).

Use of the 076 regimen also would have required a revision of the customs within many host countries where women simply do not consult a health care professional early enough in pregnancy to begin it. It also would have required intravenous administration of AZT during delivery, and in most regions of the host countries there are no facilities for such intravenous administration.

Finally, with the exception of Thailand, women in the host countries where the trials are taking place, breast-feed their newborn babies even when they know they have HIV. The transmission of HIV infection through breast-feeding is approximately 14 percent. The fact is, providing these mothers with alternatives to breast-feeding may put their infants at an even higher risk of death: Infant formula is unavailable in these countries and, even if it were available, mixing the formula with the local water could be fatal. Much of the water in these countries is contaminated with, among other things, the pathogens that cause a deadly infant diarrheal syndrome. In the regions in which the short-duration regimen of AZT was being evaluated, particularly in sub-Saharan Africa, deaths from infant diarrheal syndromes about 4 million per year.

It is clear that the 076 regimen of AZT cannot be made available to most HIV-infected pregnant women in resource-poor countries, either now or in the foreseeable future. We must find methods to reduce perinatal transmission of HIV that are within the financial and practical reach of these countries. This was the primary justification for conducting clinical trials of the short-duration regimen of AZT. The cost of the AZT in this regimen was about 10 percent of the cost of the 076 regimen. Moreover, there was no need for intravenous therapy or administration of the drug to the babies.

At the time the trials began, it seemed likely that two of the countries could afford to provide the short-duration regimen if it should prove effective, and international agencies had committed themselves to assisting the other resource-poor countries in obtaining the drug.

REDEFINING 'THE BEST'

Let us now consider whether the "best proven therapeutic method" standard for clinical trials should mean the best therapy available anywhere in the world or the standard that prevails in the host country. Guidance on this point can be found in International Ethical Guidelines prepared by CIOMS in collaboration with WHO (1993).

Unlike any other international document, the guidelines explicitly address the problems of multinational research and offers guidelines that are far superior to informed consent and other traditional protections in terms of preventing the exploitation of people in developing countries. According to the document, research sponsored by an agency in an industrialized country and carried out in a developing country must be responsive to the health needs and the priorities of the host country or community. And, in addition, any product developed in the course of such research must be made reasonably available to the inhabitants of the host country. This requirement focuses multinational research on the needs of the country in which the research is being carried out. For instance, it would eliminate conducting Phase I drug studies in Africa simply because they are less expensive and less vigorously regulated in that country.

The CIOMS guidelines also provide an important commentary on the Declaration of Helsinki:

> [T]he Declaration does not provide for controlled clinical trials. Rather, it assures the freedom of the physician 'to use a new diagnostic and therapeutic measure, if, in his or her judgment it offers hope of saving life, reestablishing health or alleviating suffering' (Article II.1). Also in regard to Phase II and Phase III drug trials there are customary and ethically justified exceptions to the requirements of the Declaration of Helsinki. A placebo given to a control group, for example, cannot be justified by its 'potential diagnostic or therapeutic value for the patient,' as Article II.6 prescribes . . . .

A research program cannot be considered the same as establishing an entitlement to the best therapy available anywhere in the world; the relevant standard is the one prevailing in the host country (Levine, 1998). It would be improper to withhold anything that is generally available in the host country in order to conduct research designed to evaluate something else.

A NEW ETHICAL STANDARD

A new ethical standard now emerging for international research is called the "highest attainable and sustainable therapeutic method" standard. "Highest attainable" means that, under the circumstances of the clinical trial, the therapy should be the best one can provide. The therapy generally available in the host country should not be considered sufficient. Instead, it should be considered the least ethically acceptable therapy.

"Sustainable" means a level of treatment that one reasonably can expect the host country can maintain relying only on its own resources after the extra resources provided by sponsors from industrialized countries are no longer available. Sustainability then serves as a constraint on "highest attainable." If that level of therapy is not sustainable, the results of the trial may not be responsive to the needs and priorities of the host country, and its therapeutic product may not be available to the inhabitants of the host country.

Providing therapy that is not sustainable may distort the research setting to the extent that the results may not be applicable in the host country.

The "highest attainable and sustainable therapeutic method" standard is reflected in the near-final draft of the *UNAIDS Guidance Document* (Joint United Nations Programme, 2000) for the conduct of multinational trials of HIV-prevention vaccine, as well as in the current draft of the revised International Ethical Guidelines. (A closely related standard is reflected in the current draft revision of the Declaration of Helsinki.)

This standard also should be used in selecting some of the therapies to be evaluated and treatments that would be made available to subjects in resource-poor countries in the course of the clinical trials.

To illustrate, let us consider a clinical trial of a new HIV-preventive vaccine in a resource-poor country. It is assumed that the vaccine will not prevent infection, only prevent or retard the progression from infection to clinical disease. Consequently, in a field trial of the vaccine, the primary outcome measure is likely to be some manifestation of disease resulting from HIV infection.

Now suppose that at the time this vaccine trial is initiated, the standard of care in industrialized countries is to administer a course of antiretroviral drugs to health care workers who have occupational exposures to HIV—a treatment known as postexposure prophylaxis (PEP). But the cost of such PEP means that treatment could not be sustained after the trial was concluded. Is it morally obligatory to provide PEP to participants in this vaccine trial?

PEP could be required ethically if the criterion were only the "highest attainable." However, because PEP is not sustainable, it would appear that it is not ethically required. Also, if PEP were provided to subjects in the vaccine trial, and if it were highly effective in preventing the progression of HIV infection to disease, there would be so few "primary outcomes" that one might never learn whether the vaccine is effective. If it were merely moderately effective in delaying progression to clinical disease, one would question whether the data derived from the vaccine trial are truly relevant to disease prevention in the country in which the trial was conducted.

The reason that provision of antiretroviral PEP is not morally obligatory is related primarily to its lack of sustainability, and not merely to the possibility that it might reduce the efficiency of the trial by decreasing the number of outcome events. (This is necessarily a simplistic analysis of the justification for PEP. A thorough ethical analysis, which is beyond the scope of this article, would entail examining the ethical standards embodied in the *UNAIDS Guidance Document* and other publications.) Counseling research subjects about reducing behaviors that increase their risk of HIV infection could similarly reduce the efficiency of vaccine trials by decreasing the number of outcome events. However, because research subjects in resource-poor countries can be counseled after the vaccine trials have been completed, it is generally ethically required to provide counseling during the course of vaccine trials.

Those who insist that Helsinki Article II.3 requires providing the best-proven therapeutic method available in industrialized countries when research is carried out in resource-poor countries must understand the implications of this position. In our case study trials of the AZT regimen in preventing perinatal transmission of HIV, most resource-poor countries could not afford to purchase sufficient AZT to implement the best therapeutic method (i.e., the 076 regimen). To truly provide the best, we also would need to include infant formula as an alternative to breast-feeding, a water supply that is safe for infants, and facilities for intravenous administration of drugs. Providing all of these "extras" would cost far more than the AZT.

Clearly, the cost of the 076 regimen is beyond the reach of most resource-poor countries. Insisting on this standard would accomplish nothing other than to deny to them the possibility of developing therapies and preventions they can afford. It would even prevent the participation of industrialized sponsors and investigators in helping them develop affordable treatments and preventions.

Application of the "highest attainable and sustainable therapeutic method" standard is, in all its respects, a more suitable ethical standard. One of its chief advantages is that it helps resource-poor countries develop needed therapies and preventions that are within their financial reach. Until the imbalances in the distribution of wealth among the nations of the world are corrected, this appears to be the best that we can do.

REFERENCES

Angell, M. 1997. The ethics of clinical research in the third world. *New England Journal of Medicine,* 337:847-849.

CIOMS (Council of International Organizations of Medical Sciences) and WHO (World Health Organization). 1993. *International Ethical Guidelines for Biomedical Research Involving Human Subjects.* Geneva, Switzerland: CIOMS.

Joint United Nations Programme on HIV/AIDS. 2000. *UNAIDS Guidance Document: Ethical Considerations in HIV Preventive Vaccine Research.* Geneva, Switzerland: UNAIDS.

Levine, RJ. 1979. Clarifying the concepts of research ethics. *Hastings Center Report,* 9(3):21-26.

——. 1988. *Ethics and Regulation of Clinical Research.* (2nd ed.) New Haven, CT: Yale University Press.

——. 1994. The impact of HIV infection on society's perception of clinical trials. *Kennedy Institute of Ethics Journal.* 4(2):93-98.

——. 1996. International codes and guidelines for research ethics: A critical appraisal. In *The Ethics of Research Involving Human Subjects: Facing the 21st Century,* Vanderpool HY, ed. Frederick, MD: University Publishing Group.

——. 1998. The "best-proven therapeutic method" standard in clinical trials in technologically developing countries, *IRB: A Review of Human Subjects Research,* 20(1): 5-9.

——. 1999. The need to revise the Declaration of Helsinki. *New England Journal of Medicine,* 341:531-534.

Lurie P, Wolfe, SM. 1997. Unethical trials of interventions to reduce perinatal transmission of the human immunodeficiency virus in developing countries. *New England Journal of Medicine,* 337:853-856.

National Commission for the Protection of Human Subjects of Biomedical and Behavioral research, 1979. *The Belmont Report: Ethical Principles and Guidelines for the Protection of Human Subjects of Research.* Washington, DC: Government Printing Office.

President's Commission for the Study of Ethical Problems in Medicine and Biomedical and Behavioral Research. 1981. *Protecting Human Subjects: The Adequacy and Uniformity of Federal Rules and Their Implementation.* Washington, DC: Government Printing Office.

BREAKING DOWN EDUCATION AND PRACTICE BARRIERS

10. Globalization: Opportunities for International Standards

RICHARD L. O'BRIEN

JANUARY 1, 1994. THE NORTH AMERICAN FREE TRADE Agreement (NAFTA) is in effect. Ross Perot has issued his warning about "a giant sucking sound" of jobs going south. Chapter 12 of NAFTA commits the United States, Canada, and Mexico to removing permanent residency and citizenship from the eligibility requirements for licensure in the professions. Licensing is to be based on fair, objective, and transparent criteria. Standards for admission to licensure exams may not be inequitably burdensome. Each nation is committed to recognizing quality education in the other NAFTA signatories.

Some health professionals and academic health centers now fear that the giant sucking sound will be made by students going south, and that the roar of an incoming tide of foreign professionals will soon be heard in the land. Like broom factories and auto assembly plants, new health professions schools will spring up in Mexico and Canada to attract American students with low-cost tuitions. There will be a sudden and rapid influx of immigrant professionals from Mexico and Canada, determined to reap the benefits of the American standard of living and high incomes. The already-precarious balance between U.S. need for professionals and the U.S. institutions to educate them will be further destabilized. These are only a few of the fears engendered by the prospect of a more open, Pan-American market in the health care field.

NAFTA is one of several treaties intended to facilitate not only international trade but also the international movement and services of professionals. The European Union has removed barriers to free movement of professionals across its international boundaries and established mutual recognition of education credentials. The General Agreement on Trade in Services (GATS), signed by World Trade Organization (WTO) members, clearly expresses the same intent; it actually has created schedules for removing barriers to the provision of services and movement of professionals across international borders.

THE RELENTLESS MARCH TOWARD GLOBALIZATION

There is no doubt that we now live in a global village, a community in which events in Thailand are felt within weeks or months in London markets, one in which the Russian ruble and the entire economy upon which it is founded are brought down by real estate speculation in Malaysia. The Golden Arches of McDonald's and the Kentucky Fried Chicken signs are everywhere. The worldwide distribution of American movies is of sufficient magnitude to induce some countries to enact laws banning them in an effort to counter the "cultural threat" they pose.

The march toward globalization is relentless, driven by people's desires for better lives and higher standards of living. It is facilitated by the continuing and accelerating (r)evolution of worldwide access to information. Human beings are in constant search of fuller, healthier, richer lives. When people in one place realize that people elsewhere live better than they do, they inevitably aspire to share in that better life. Globalization is not solely an economic or trade phenomenon. It is a convergence of cultures, an increasing similarity between the lives and aspirations of diverse peoples.

Globalization began when Homo erectus first walked out of familiar territory. The history of humanity is a process of continuous cultural evolution and adaptation to different environments. For millennia, this process has resulted in the differentiation and divergence of cultures. Although cultural exchange has always been with us, the spread of humanity and cultural adaptation to local environments has outpaced the effects of interactions between diverging populations.

Two forces, both resulting from technology development, have changed the evolutionary process of cultural divergence, not suddenly but slowly. Humanity's increasing control over the environment and the accelerating pace of transportation, communication, and information exchange has led to more frequent and longer interactions between cultures. At some point and at different times in different places, cultures that had been diverging and differentiating began to converge and to adopt characteristics of other cultures. As divergent cultures become more similar, they evolve a new, blended culture that incorporates the most adaptive and desired features of all the societies that came before.

FEAR OF CONVERGENCE

Cultural convergence is often threatening, evoking fears of homogenization, erosion of values, or encroachment of alien values. Nonetheless, all cultures evolve as adaptations to their environments. Convergence is inevitable. Most evolved cultures are amalgams resulting from interactions and clashes, followed by accommodation and integration, and finally merging into a new blend that preserves those features of each culture that best suit the time and place. Cultures develop to suit peoples' needs and desires. They survive as long as they meet those needs, and change (or die) when they do not.

Some people equate globalization with Americanization. Indeed, American products and popular culture have strong worldwide appeal. Many scientific and technological advances originate in the United States, and our economy is a dominant force in the world marketplace. The United States has been a model of the good life for many peoples of the world for at least a century. It continues to be the nation most favored for immigration.

Conversely, it may be argued that American culture is a result of globalization. The United States is the product of multiple influences brought to this country by diverse cultures from around the globe. North America is a locus of merging cultures. We are "globalized" by immigrants and visitors. We are a conduit through which numerous evolving cultures flow to other parts of the world to influence the very cultures that engendered them.

This model of cultural spread is rather different from those that preceded it. Renaissance Italy and France developed cultural traits adopted by other nations. British and Spanish colonialism, on the other hand, ignored native cultures rather than adopting and synthesizing them. From the colonial perspective, "going native" was frowned upon; the colonists avoided adopting the cultural traits of the colonized peoples at all costs.

In the past, the spread of culture has most commonly been achieved (and resisted) by military conflict. However, that pattern is at last happily shifting as more and more nations come to realize that security is best achieved by cooperation, not by conflict. This is the impetus behind trade treaties. Governments attempt to facilitate and regulate globalization to protect the interests of their citizens. Regulation may impede globalization by imposing barriers to trade and the movement of persons, but globalization will continue to advance. It is a natural human phenomenon that will occur, regardless of efforts to facilitate or impede it.

BARRIERS TO THE GLOBALIZATION OF HEALTH

Health professions and professional education are as susceptible to globalizing trends as are the other facets of our life, but free international trade in professional services and education has encountered substantial barriers. Although many people continue to fear the economic consequences of free trade, the fact is that 6 years after NAFTA, there is little clear evidence of its effects on American health professions and education. Barriers apparently include language and culture, different definitions of professional boundaries, and restrictions on immigration and emigration.

One of the most substantial barriers to free trade in the health professions is the legitimate concern about consistency in the quality of education and competence of professionals. Most nations control and regulate professional services and education tightly in the effort to assure quality and competence. Nations are reluctant to accept educational accreditation or professional certification by other nations, and some countries refuse it outright.

People seeking professional licensure or admission to foreign schools frequently encounter special requirements, including citizenship, residency, or additional education.

Despite these barriers, there is a substantial international trade in health services and health professions education. Patients travel across international borders for treatment. Students study in other countries. Health professionals migrate across national boundaries. The United States, in particular, is a substantial net exporter of health services as well as an importer of knowledge and immigrant professionals, especially nurses and physicians.

Free trade in professional services and education is facilitated by trade agreements, which offer health care professionals an opportunity to raise the quality of clinical practice and education worldwide. As a correlation, consider the ways in which international trade has enhanced the quality of automobile production. The development of high standards of performance and reliability, largely by Japanese automakers, has induced American and European automakers to improve their products so that they are competitive. This suggests that the same can and will occur within the health care field.

SETTING INTERNATIONAL STANDARDS: AN OBJECT LESSON

To ensure high international standards of quality internationally in the field of health care services and education, it is imperative that we develop international standards of professional competence and educational quality. American health professions, in general, and the Association of Academic Health Centers (AHC), in particular, can make major contributions to developing such standards.

Academic health centers in this country are the storehouses of scientific, technical, and cultural advances in health care and health professions education. These institutions have played a crucial role in developing uniform standards for professional licensure, certification, and educational accreditation.

The American experience also can serve as an object lesson in how to avoid or overcome roadblocks to developing such standards. The fact is that

American standards have evolved very slowly. It has taken this country's medical establishment nearly a century and a half to develop uniform standards of practice and education.

IN THE U.S.: THE SLOW TREK TOWARD MEDICAL UNIFORMITY

The practice of medicine was unregulated in the United States until the middle of the 19th century. In 1846, North Carolina became the first state to require professional licensure to practice medicine. Other states eventually followed, each with its own registration and licensure requirements. Certain types of medical practices were reserved by law to licensed or registered physicians. Standards were developed to assure quality and protect the public from bad practice. By the end of the 19th century, most (but not all) states required an examination to obtain a license to practice medicine. Some admitted to practice only graduates from a limited list of state-approved schools.

Each state had its own procedure for licensure, but these varied widely and were of inconsistent quality. The diverse standards imposed significant burdens on physicians and often were unrelated to the quality of education and practice. Eventually, physicians throughout the United States demanded professional mobility and the ability to practice in other states. Their pressure led to the development of more uniform standards and programs for reciprocal licensure.

In 1912, the Federation of State Medical Boards (FSMB) was created to assure consistency and high standards for licensure. It was established by the merger of two organizations, the National Confederation of State Medical Examining and Licensing Boards (est. 1891), and the American Confederation of Reciprocating Examining and Licensing Boards (est. 1902); each promulgated greater national consistency in licensing standards. The National Board of Medical Examiners (NBME) was established in 1915 to develop examinations that would require national standards of competence for medical licensure and practice.

Acceptance of the National Board examinations was slow. States found many reasons to maintain their own examinations or reject the National

Board exams. However, by the 1960s, most states accepted all or part of the NBME exams for licensure. In addition, many states reciprocally recognized other's state exams (indicating that the state exams themselves had improved substantially), thereby allowing professional competence to be assessed on the basis of consistent standards.

In 1968, FSMB and NBME developed the Federation Licensing Examination (FLEX) to achieve greater uniformity of examinations. By the early 1970s, FLEX was used and recognized by all states and certain other jurisdictions. National Board exams continued to be offered and accepted by most states; meanwhile, FLEX continued to evolve.

In the long process of developing uniform licensure standards, the United States encountered the need to think globally to assure the quality of foreign nationals wishing to practice in the United States. In 1956, long before the United States agreed under NAFTA to abolish citizenship and residency requirements for professional licensure, the United States established the Education Commission on Foreign Medical Graduates (ECFMG) to assure the quality of physicians entering the United States to practice. In 1992, the United States Medical Licensure Exam (USMLE) emerged from the NBME, FLEX, and ECFMG examination procedures. It is now the sole U.S.-accepted certification and examination procedure and the single pathway to medical licensure in the United States.

STRIVING FOR UNIFORMITY IN OTHER HEALTH PROFESSIONS

Thus, it took from 1846 to 1992 for the United States to develop uniform procedures and standards for medical licensure. Even now, there are health professions without uniform standards accepted in all states. Let us examine a few of these health professions.

Nursing

Nursing followed a path similar to that of medicine. In 1903, North Carolina became the first state to require examination and registration for nurses. Other states followed, many requiring graduation from approved training programs. As in medicine, each state had its own licensing examination and procedures.

In 1942, the National League for Nursing Education recommended that all states adopt a uniform set of examination standards. In 1944, the State Board Test Pool (SBTP) was established, and 15 states began to use these examinations. By 1950, all 48 states, the District of Columbia, and the Territory of Hawaii were using the same examination for licensure. However, until 1970, 20 states still did not require licensure to practice nursing. In the 1980s, the National Council License Examination (NCLEX) replaced the SBTP.

Nursing also responded to the need to assure competence of immigrant professionals. As a result of a 1975 Department of Health, Education, and Welfare conference, the Commission on Graduates of Foreign Nursing Schools was established to certify that graduates of foreign nursing educational programs are qualified to sit for licensure examinations.

Accreditation

The evolution of uniform standards of accreditation in professional education followed a similar process. In 1847, the American Medical Association (AMA) was founded. Its members immediately established the Council on Medical Education whose primary purpose was to develop and apply standards of medical education. In 1890, 66 medical school deans formed the Association of American Medical Colleges (AAMC) with the purpose of reforming medical education. By the early 20th century, both the AMA and AAMC accredited educational programs awarding medical degrees. Most schools that survived the aftermath of the Flexner report submitted to the burden of accreditation by both entities.

Including Canada in Accreditation

In 1942, the medical education accreditation standards and processes of the AMA and AAMC were merged, and the Liaison Committee on Medical Education (LCME) was formed. A step toward internationalization occurred in the early 1960s when the LCME began to accredit Canadian schools. The Council on Accreditation of Canadian Medical Schools was formed in 1979 to involve Canadian schools formally in the accreditation process and to define specific Canadian societal needs. It offered a process that applied the same accreditation standards to all medical schools in the United States and Canada.

Thus, for approximately 150 years, we have been engaged in developing widely used and universally recognized standards of professional education and professional practice. The primary motivation has been to assure universal quality. In addition, these standards have simplified the licensure process and diminished the burden of adhering to diverse standards and processes.

The United States and Canada accomplished this feat across borders despite perceived cultural and linguistic barriers. Canadian Francophone medical schools are accredited by the same process and standards as are Canadian Anglophone and United States schools. Francophone graduates meet the same or similar licensure requirements as do the graduates of anglophone schools.

Accommodating linguistic and cultural differences has not been unique to Canada. Florida, for example, has a large Spanish-speaking population. This state recently developed an examination that is being translated into Spanish for physicians who are Spanish-speaking refugees. Given the changing face of the United States, it soon may be necessary to translate examinations into other languages as well. The challenge will be to translate accurately without compromising the quality of licensure standards. Standards need not be compromised. The Canadian experience demonstrates that it is feasible to apply comparable or uniform standards across languages and cultures.

North America has led the world in developing universal standards for professional licensure, accreditation, and the certification of specialty practices not only in medicine and nursing but also in almost all other health professions. The development and acceptance of uniform standards has not been easy. It has taken more than a century of medicine to achieve standardization within our own borders, an effort slowed down by individual state efforts to restrict and retain control over the flow of incoming professionals across state boundaries. For years, national standardization had to grapple with the conviction of individual states that "We are doing this well; why change?"

Most of the rest of the world has begun to follow a similar path toward universal standards. In most nations, professional education is governmentally sponsored and certified, usually by a Ministry of Education or its equivalent. Until recently, few other countries had a formalized process of self-study and peer review evolved in the United States.

In most nations, graduation from a government-approved educational institution has been deemed adequate evidence of competence. Professionals were, and in some nations still are, registered to practice after receiving a professional degree rather than after being assessed for individual competence. In the last 10 to 15 years, other nations, though late in the process, have made strong commitments to developing uniform standards of education and practice. Increasingly, more nations are coming to recognize the importance of developing mutually acceptable international standards of practice and education.

Although the benefit of developing international standards of practice and education is widely accepted, there continue to be many real, potential, and perceived barriers to progress. The same kind of impediments that slowed down standardization in North America also exist globally. Additional barriers also come into play, such as significant cultural differences, including professional and linguistic differences and divergent definitions of professional boundaries. Many countries also have a strong antipathy to what they perceive to be American cultural arrogance or cultural imperialism.

IMPROVING HEALTH AND EDUCATION WORLDWIDE

The Board on International Health of the Institute of Medicine (IOM, 1997) has published *America's Vital Interest in Global Health,* a book that makes a very strong case for the importance of global health and the U.S. ability and responsibility to foster it. It specifically refers to the high quality of education and practice in the United States and charges us to play a role in improving health and education globally.

Several initiatives are now underway to establish international standards of practice and education. Some result from trade agreements, others from professional recognition of opportunity or need. Some examples follow.

- NAFTA has fostered the Trilateral Initiative in nursing, which has established goals for developing uniform or mutually acceptable standards of nursing education and licensure in Canada, Mexico, and the United States.
- The International Federation of Nurse Anesthetists, whose members comprise professional societies in 32 nations, has established international standards for nurse anesthesia programs, including required competencies, standards of practice, and a code of ethics.
- The Federation of State Medical Boards is participating with representatives from eight other nations (mostly English-speaking) in a discussion leading to the formation of an International Association of Medical Licensing Authorities to develop international licensing standards.
- Eighteen Caribbean nations have formed the Caribbean Association of Medical Councils (CAMC) to develop and administer a regional examination that will allow those who pass to practice in any of the CAMC nations. By the year 2004, all medical personnel who want to practice in a member nation will be required to pass this exam.
- A number of nations in Europe and Latin America have consulted with the LCME about developing their accreditation procedures and standards for medical education. Mexico has applied LCME standards to review and accredit 12 of its 58 medical schools.
- Specialty organizations have begun to develop international standards of education and certification. Thoracic surgeons have developed a standard international training curriculum. Cardiologists and cardiothoracic surgeons have adopted international standards for coronary revascularization. Also now under consideration are standards for valve surgery.
- The Accreditation Council for Graduate Medical Education (ACGME) Residency Review Committees and the Canadian Royal College of Physicians are discussing the development of uniform standards of program accreditation. American specialty boards and the Canadian Royal College of Physicians have begun to develop common requirements for certification and recertification.
- Because California (like some other states) faces a shortage of den-

tists that cannot be met by graduates, the California Assembly Bill 1116 has mandated the Board of Dental Examiners to develop a plan to accredit foreign dental schools based on prescribed standards and procedures.

Cultural differences may result in an inability to find completely common ground regarding uniform standards and procedures. In instances where harmonization (such as identical standards and procedures) cannot be achieved, we must be prepared to recognize so that quality may be assessed by appropriately different means meet the cultural needs of other nations.

As we strive to enhance the internationalization of the health professions education and the development of high standards of practice, we must take care to do so with humility. We must recognize that other nations expect cooperation and collaboration rather than an imposition of standards and procedures. We must be willing to learn from others, to change our procedures to adapt to their needs, and to adopt what they contribute.

We must tread lightly. Although we have a long history of excellent higher education, we do not have a monopoly on quality. In fact, for more than a century, acquiring at least part of one's education in Europe was highly sought after. It was considered by many in the United States to be evidence of quality. We must never forget that many contributions to professional practice, education, scientific knowledge, and technology come to us from other nations.

GLOBAL EDUCATION: EXPLORING NEW OPPORTUNITIES

Globalization and technology present great educational opportunities to U.S. academic health centers above and beyond opportunities for standardizing professional practice and education internationally. As an example, let us consider the case of Boris M., a graduate of the Moscow State University Faculty of Medicine. Boris has taken and passed USMLE Parts I and II, has taken and passed the ECFMG English language proficiency test, and has passed the clinical skills assessment. He holds an ECFMG certificate. He has not applied for graduate medical education in the United States, nor does he intend to emigrate here. He has become ECFMG-certified because it attests to his educational attainment, provides recognition that he has achieved a high level of professional competence, and confers status. It will assist him in the development and advancement in his medical career in Russia.

The World Wide Web also provides a great opportunity for the global provision of health professions education. With the continued expansion of technology and distance education, professional education has become an international commodity. There is strong demand for American health professions education in many parts of the world. For instance, Creighton University has received inquiries and requests for an Internet-mediated pharmacy and nursing education from Australia, Turkey, the Middle East, and several eastern and western European nations. Other American universities have also received requests.

As standards of education and certification become internationalized, opportunities will arise to attract certifiably well-educated and competent professionals to our faculties. There is already international traffic in faculty members with strong track records of professional competence and research productivity. This market promises to open further, facilitating recruitment of qualified faculty members from the entire world that, in turn, will create opportunities abroad for American professionals.

Globalization and the development of international standards for accreditation and certification will offer academic health centers more and more opportunities to export their expertise and experience to other nations. Is the opportunity accompanied by threats? Those who trade in goods recognize that international treaties that remove barriers to trade frequently result in manufacturers moving production facilities to lower-cost, off-shore sites. Is it possible or likely that the establishment of international education standards will result in the development of health professions educational institutions abroad that attract students now matriculating at U.S. health professions schools?

For decades, Americans have had ample opportunities to study health professions abroad. Those pursuing these opportunities are generally (but not exclusively) people who fail to gain admission to programs in the United States. Their success rate is much lower than that of graduates from U.S. schools, and their numbers have not been large. Ross Perot's prediction of a giant sucking sound—in our case, of students rushing south—has simply not occurred nor is it likely to. Rather, the development of international education standards may, and should, elevate educational quality at the international institutions from which we now import professionals. Recall the attrition of American medical schools after the Flexner report and the establishment of the AAMC and AMA accreditation systems.

In the marketplace of educational services, as in the marketplace of goods, quality and value will determine the winners. This nation's history of developing quality assurance should give us a sense of security about globalization. We should have a sense of responsibility toward fostering such globalization, particularly because the process has enormous potential to improve health care and health professions education worldwide.

REFERENCES

Bobby, CL. 1999. In *Strategies for Change and Improvement: The report of the Task Force on Accreditation of Health Professions Education*, SB Gelman, EH O'Neil, and JR Kimmey, eds. San Francisco, CA: UCSF Center for Health Professions, pp. 58-63. Available from URL: *http://futurehealth.ucsf.edu/pdf_files/accredit.pdf*

Commission on Graduates of Foreign Nursing Schools. *The Trilateral Initiative on North American Nursing. 1996. Philadelphia, PA: CGFNS.* Available from URL: *http://www.cgnus.org/trilateral/trilater.htm*

Friedman, TL. 1999. *The Lexus and the Olive Tree.* New York, NY: Farrar Straus Giroux.

Hubbard, JP and Levit, EJ. 1985. *The National Board of Medical Examiners: The First Seventy Years.* Philadelphia, PA: NBME.

International Federation of Nurse Anesthetists. Available from URL: *http://home.swipnet.se/nw-37510/IFNA.html*

IOM (Institute of Medicine) Board on International Health. 1997. America's Vital Interest in Global Health. Washington, DC: National Academy Press. Available from URL: *http://bob.nap.edu/readingroom/books/avi*

Lenn, MP and Miller, BD, eds. 1999. *The Foundations of Higher Education and the Professions.* Washington, DC: The Center for Quality Assurance in International Education.

Petersen, JC. 1999. *Internationalizing Quality Assurance in Higher Education.* Washington, DC: Council for Higher Education Accreditation.

11. Inter-American Collaboration in Health Professions Education

PABLO A. PULIDO

COUNTRIES IN LATIN AMERICA AND THE CARIBBEAN have tremendous strategic importance to the United States with the potential to have a significant impact on the everyday lives of U.S. citizens.[1] However, until recently, Latin American was largely overlooked until some political crisis, social upheaval, or natural disaster captured our attention. With the advent of the new technologies that speed information around the world, the United States no longer can ignore Latin America, particularly in the areas of education and health care.

[1] For example, the North American Free Trade Agreement (NAFTA), MercoSur (Southern Common Market, comprising Argentina, Paraguay, Uruguay, and Brazil), and the developing CariCom (Caribbean Community) are creating new major trade environments. More than 50 percent of all oil imported to the United States comes from Latin America (Mosbacher, 1999) and Venezuela alone is the major U.S. energy supplier.

DEFINING LATIN AMERICA

Latin America encompasses the inhabitants of the southern hemisphere. The Spanish-speaking population to the south of the United States extends beyond Central and South America as follows:

1. Spanish NAFTA–Total population: 135,881,000. Includes Mexico (98,881,000) and Spanish-speaking U.S. citizens (37,000,000). They are not traditionally considered to be Latin American.
2. Spanish Central and Caribbean America–Total population: 52,950,000. Includes Costa Rica (4,023,000), Cuba (11,201,000), El Salvador (6,276,000), Guatemala (11,385,000), Honduras (6,485,000), Nicaragua (5,074,000), and the Dominican Republic (8,495,000).
3. Andean Group–Total population: 104,610,000. Includes Colombia (42,321,000), Ecuador (12,460,000), Peru (25,662,000), and Venezuela (24,170,000).
4. MercoSur (Southern Common Market)–Total population: 240,100,000). Includes Argentina (37,032,000), Bolivia (8,329,000), Brazil (170,693,000), Chile (15,211,000), Paraguay (5,496,000), and Uruguay (3,337,000).

These Spanish-speaking people (about 8 percent of the global population) live in Spanish-, Portuguese-, English-, Dutch-, and French-speaking communities within a geographical area of approximately 20 million square kilometers. Many suffer from substantial unmet needs in health, education, nutrition, employment, and housing. Hope vanished long ago that outsiders would intervene miraculously to solve them (Landes, 1998), and they are now facing reality head-on and implementing dynamic and dramatic economic changes.

Argentina has the highest gross domestic product (GDP) per capita in Latin America, at $8,860 per year. MercoSur has the fourth largest integrated market in the world after NAFTA, the European Union, and Japan. Brazil is the economic powerhouse of the Latin American continent, with a GDP of 676 billion dollars a year. It is also the tenth largest economy in the world.

A wealthy economic corridor extends from sea to sea, reaching from the cities of Valparaiso and Santiago on the Pacific coast of Chile, through the cities of Mendoza, Cordoba, Rosario, and Buenos Aires in Argentina, to the Atlantic coast of Brazil, including such urban centers as Porto Alegre, Belo Horizonte, São Paulo, and Rio de Janeiro. This economic and cultural corridor, called "El Dorado," has a population of 110 million people and a per capita income similar to that of Italy. It contains regions of great agricultural prosperity and advanced technological development. Over the past decade, it also has attracted most of the foreign development in the continent.

A significant change has been the growing population and shifting demographics. People are moving from rural areas into towns. As a result, the existing health care systems, which were designed for a rural population, must adapt to meet the needs of increasingly overcrowded cities. A further critical issue is the shift from a predominantly young to an increasingly elderly population. The region's medical and health education and services have not been geared toward meeting the needs of older patients.

In addition, health care expenditures are diminishing and used inefficiently (World Bank, 1993, 1995, 1998). A high percentage of the Latin American labor force works in the public sector that, with very few exceptions, is controlled by political systems, all too often overstaffed with invisible, unproductive employees and riddled with inefficiency, mediocrity, and corruption. The percentage (4 percent) spent on health, at least in the public sector in Latin America, is less than half that spent in major economies (9.2 percent) (World Bank, 1993). It is only slightly higher than that of the former socialist economies in Europe. The mean Latin American per capita health expenditure is US$105. Worse yet, these expenditures are dispersed through a system characterized by inefficient management, reducing the available money drastically as it passes from the central government to the regional and municipal authorities.

THE GOLDEN AGE OF HEALTH CARE

The "golden sixties and seventies" of Inter-American collaboration were characterized by a strong belief in hemispheric partnership. The social and economic development for all the nations of the Americas was a political and social goal. The Kennedy Administration's Alliance for Progress, an unprecedented and ambitious program of socioeconomic development, sought to build solid economic infrastructures and strengthen intellectual leadership throughout the hemisphere.

It was in this climate of hemispheric solidarity that the Federacion Panamericana de Asociaciones de Facultades y Escuelas de Medicina (PAFAMS) was founded in 1962, integrating twelve national associations of medical schools and nine affiliated institutions. It was formed at the instigation of the Association of American Medical Colleges (AAMC), the Association of Canadian Medical Colleges (CMAC), and the Colombian Association of Medical Schools (ASCOFAME), with support from other national associations and individual schools throughout the hemisphere.

The PAFAMS is a private, nonprofit, academic, nongovernmental organization dedicated to the advancement of medical education and the biomedical sciences in the Americas. Its primary mission is to promote and improve medical education throughout the continent. Known as the Federacion Panamericana de Asociaciones de Facultades y Escuelas de Medicina (FEPAFEM) in Spanish, it now includes more than 350 medical schools throughout Latin America, with approximately 50,000 faculty members and 450,000 students.

The PAFAMS places a strong emphasis upon improving universities. Holding that the population's health, quality of life, and productivity can best be improved by training a cadre of well-qualified health professionals, it provides decisive national and international support for improving academics to various medical schools. In addition, the organization fosters many sister and collaborative North-South programs, all of which elevate the standards of professional and technical education and health care throughout Latin America.

As a result, excellent new medical schools have been created and existing institutions have improved dramatically. Many physicians, nurses, and other health care practitioners have received advanced training both at North American institutions and in selected Latin American centers that have risen to new levels of academic excellence.

The "golden years" also strengthened the sense of social responsibility for many academic health centers. It was during this period that the true renovation (some would call it a "revolution") of medical education took place. Medical schools moved away from being "vocational institutions" whose only task was to train doctors and clinical specialists for the private practice of medicine by expanding their medical curricula to include the social and biological sciences, thereby emerging as academic institutions. Disciplines such as anthropology, sociology, and demography gained the stature of basic sciences, and public health issues took on new importance as medical schools addressed such problems as excessive population growth. Standards were upgraded for establishing and operating medical schools, most notably through a program to improve hospital accreditation and graduate school certification cosponsored by the Pan American Health Organization (PAHO) and several countries.

Such programs were made possible because of two prevailing conditions (Patiño, 1997):

- Well-defined national and international policies that treated medical education as a crucial factor in promoting socioeconomic development.
- Collaboration between North American governmental and private institutions and agencies to promote development.

FALLING INTO ISOLATIONISM

The explosive growth of medical schools in the 1960s reached a plateau in the 1970s. Unfortunately, the resulting surplus of physicians (Bankowski and Mejía, 1987) did not translate to an increase in access to medical care. The highest concentration of the medical workforce tended to be in urban areas, and the outlying areas were left without adequate health care. In the late 1970s, Latin American universities and medical schools began to lose ground. Academic excellence yielded to severe economic limitations, as well as to a form of political activism that was both ill-conceived and counterproductive. Collaborative programs all but disappeared, and the intellectual presence and leadership provided by the United States waned. New groups of specialists trained in Eastern Europe replaced U.S.-trained professionals. The value system placing academic excellence as the primary goal of a reputable university or medical school gradually faded.

This deterioration inevitably resulted in a period of crisis. In the 1980s, universities and medical schools, especially those serving the public sector, saw their academic quality deteriorate under a misguided ideal of educating students exclusively for "primary health care." Throughout the decade, there was a general disregard for academic excellence and the scientific method. As a result, research conducted by existing medical schools during this time was generally poor. At the same time, many new schools were founded without adequate resources and research facilities and graduated a disproportionately high number of physicians, effectively lopsiding the health workforce.

Toward the end of the 1980s, public health care in most of the Latin American nations was dismal. Hospitals and clinical facilities had deteriorated, research activities were almost nonexistent, health care had weakened at both the secondary and tertiary levels, and primary care coverage was extremely poor. The dissolution of Pan-American idealism, the lessening of activities, and the virtual abandonment of the "partnership for development" paradigm were unquestionably a consequence of the widespread economic crises that had spread throughout the hemisphere during the 1980s.

The price of the new climate of isolationism was the weakening of a number of internationally oriented organizations, including the Organization of American States (OAS), PAHO, the World Health Organization (WHO), and, to a certain extent, the PAFAMS. In this context, the mission of the Association of Academic Health Centers (AHC) takes on particular significance. The AHC's work is not only pertinent but also extremely important, as it promotes international communication and fosters the catalytic power of exchanging medical knowledge, workforce assets, new ideas, and experiences.

The 1990s saw a renewed strengthening of human resources. The number of medical schools in the region is now growing at a rate of 3 percent biannually. Approximately 62 percent of the medical schools are state-financed institutions although almost all of the new schools are privately funded. During the 1990s, almost all countries in the region surpassed the target of 10 physicians per 10,000 inhabitants. The Spanish-speaking region currently has 753,984 physicians, 264,000 dentists, and 355,106 auxiliary personnel. The workforce in the health sector is predominantly female—a trend that promises to continue over the next decade. In fact, throughout the region, one-third of all physicians are female.

HEALTH REFORM AND ITS CHALLENGES

Medical education throughout the hemisphere should now focus its educational programs, services, and plans on preparing health professionals to practice in the 21st century and meet the challenges of current and emerging health policies. For instance, how can we maximize access to high-quality care while containing the costs of expensive health services? How can we promote national public insurance practices via strategic alliances with private insurers to improve both for-profit and nonprofit health care? Twenty-first century health professionals must come to terms with a variety of important issues, including:

1. Only an educated workforce can make effective reforms.
2. Leadership must arise from a realistic awareness of the health care field.
3. Information technology is revolutionizing our communications capabilities.
4. Decisions should be based upon current information and databases.

Significant changes in health care delivery and medical practice demand a drastic reorientation of medical education toward promoting health and preventing disease (Evans, 1981; McGuire, 1994). Physicians and their institutions, including medical schools, must define a target for optimal care through existing primary care systems and put the new ideals into everyday practice, both in the classroom and in the clinic. International health organizations, professional societies, and individual physicians must cease regarding health merely as the absence of disease. All health professionals need to factor in biological, psychological, social, and environmental determinants of health arising from education, cultural, economic, and geopolitical concerns.

When governments express a desire to offer universal health coverage and equal access for all, they tend to do so by making declarations proclaiming "everything for health and health for all." Unfortunately, time and experience have demonstrated that such declarations do not take into account the very real effects of a nation's budget, currency fragility, external debt, inflation, speculation, and other inefficiencies that stymie efforts to improve health and upgrade health care. Another problem is the extremely expensive cost of computer equipment and software that often proves to be unwarranted in many situations (World Bank, 1993). Sadly, many developing countries invest in technology without considering the genuine benefits but because such investment it is perceived to be prestigious.

A number of low–tech basic health indicators have a serious impact upon health in Latin America. These include access to health care, the number of births attended by professionals, and the percentage of malnourished children—all issues that are inextricably bound to the economic conditions within each country (World Bank, 1993, 1995, 1998).

Despite economic pressures, some promising initiatives, such as the establishment of health foundations to manage local hospitals, are emerging. Such new initiatives promote more equity, better efficiency, and greater self-improvement. The general population pays for health services, either directly or through taxes or contributions to social welfare programs. A sharp decrease in government health services allocations has fostered the development of prepayment per capita systems.

However, there is a sharp contrast between health care financing and the actual delivery of health care services. This has serious ramifications for the education of physicians, as well as for the governments of these countries: A government has a responsibility to oversee its public institutions, as well as to expedite collaboration between private and public service providers.

DECENTRALIZATION AND ITS EFFECT ON HEALTH CARE

Several countries in Latin America are in the midst of decentralizing their governments, transferring political authority over health care services to the individual states, provinces, municipal authorities, and local governments. Colombia, for instance, plans to modify its national health system radically, proposing universal health care coverage and decentralized operational authority for health care services. The Social Security monopoly will be dissolved, and free-market competition will be introduced. The government's new and challenging role is to serve as a financial agency. This reform, which places a high priority on access and coverage, is expected to improve efficiency by reaching more of the indigent and the elderly throughout Colombia.

In Chile, the Servicios Medicos Nacionales (SERMENA) started in 1968 as a free-choice medical care insurance system (and a mutual fund for Social Security). In 1969, SERMENA established a generic drug formulary amid disputes about a united health service versus a mixed public-private system. In 1979, individual foundations were established to manage the financial aspects of health care. The National Health Foundation (FONASA) was formed from a fusion of SERMENA with the National Health Service. Signifying a major move toward decentralization, FONASA established 26 regional offices and one single environmental health service in the capital, Santiago. The local provinces now have the power to manage billing and about 25 percent of all expenditures. Financial control for investments and payroll expenditure remain centralized.

Other countries in Latin America have commenced the decentralization process by transferring political authority for the management and delivery of health services to the states or local governments (World Bank, 1993, 1995, 1998; Burki, Perry, 1998). It is a painstaking process. For instance, Venezuela's Ministry of Health restructured its system in 1993, transferring responsibility for health care institutions to the individual states. Within a controlled geopolitical area, a decentralized public health sector has become a social enterprise of the states (Pulido, 1995). The states are responsible for productivity, quality, and cost efficiency. They also must purchase basic services from private providers and establish budget control mechanisms. This revolution, which has had a powerful impact upon medical practice, also has affected medical education, requiring the formation of new financial priorities geared toward developing a successful primary care infrastructure.

CHANGES IN HEALTH PROFESSIONS EDUCATION

Until the 1960s, data collected throughout Latin America were rarely applied, resulting in widespread misunderstanding about the realities of health care. More recently, data collection has been augmented by expertise from other countries, promoting a more systematic approach to medical education. Recent improvements include more innovative teaching methods and the integration of such subjects as epidemiology and community medicine into the curriculum. Academic programs are being redesigned to achieve clinical as well as public health goals. PAFAMS also has established systems for evaluating programs and outcomes. In these and other ways, medical education has been improved, thanks to a more open exchange of ideas and experiences among PAFAMS members, associations, and affiliated medical schools.

The major improvement has been the recognition that dynamic changes are afoot to which all professionals in the health care field must remain open. Within medical education, a number of factors are serving as catalysts for change, as follows:

- Recent explosion of knowledge.
- Pervasive loss of idealism.
- Little understanding of what medicine is or should be.
- Little or no sympathy for individual human beings.
- Limited time dedicated to medical education by the faculty.
- Premature inclination towards specialization and the decline of generalism.
- Neglect of primary health care and the needs of local communities.
- Reallocated economic resources and personnel.
- Use of physical facilities, hospitals, and ambulatory settings as arenas in which to practice and develop medical education.
- Redefinition of educational priorities in terms of national policies.
- Development of health service centers versus academic centers.
- Use of the community as a resource to reinforce its capacities and provide solutions for the problems of the community.
- Admissions policies of medical schools.
- Promotion of public education on health issues.
- Study of the impact of social sciences on health services.
- Emergence of new issues and disciplines such as ethics, epidemiology, and health economics.

The standards of quality in Latin American medical schools range from excellent (schools with high standards in admission and research) to abysmal (schools with open admission, marginal concern for critical issues, and few resources to support academic and nonacademic activities). National accreditation systems are not yet in place in Latin America, although attempts in this direction are being made by the National Associations of Medical Schools.

There are significant disparities in the quality of education between institutions accepted by the Country Association of Medical Schools (CAMS, an affiliate of PAFAMS), and for-profit schools that are more commercially oriented. In Colombia, 24 institutions are recognized by CAMS, while 20 are still new and not yet recognized. In Costa Rica, only 1 institution is recognized against seven that are not. CAMS recognizes 58 schools in México, but another 15 remain unrecognized. This paucity of CAMS-approved schools has a particularly negative impact upon the more rural districts: Outlying communities have a pressing need for primary care, as well as social and community services.

To deal with this dilemma, PAHO has sponsored a project conducted by the Regional Library of Medicine in São Paolo (Biblioteca Regional de Medicina), now called the Latin American and Caribbean Center for Health Sciences Information. The center has developed a cadre of librarians and information scholars in Colombia, Chile, Venezuela, and other countries in Latin America. With support from the National Library of Medicine in the United States, these professionals are building an electronic communication network connecting PAHO and PAFAMS schools. This network facilitates the exchange of information about the latest innovations in medical education.

In Latin America and elsewhere throughout the world, academic health centers are coming to rely more and more upon databases to keep medical education and health care delivery systems up-to-date and effective. Latin American academic health centers also seek to meet the needs of their rural communities by promoting more community-based educational programs and services. These medical social services programs are by no means new; the first were introduced in Mexico in 1936 (Bankowski & Mejía, 1987). These programs help young clinicians develop the communication skills and cultural sensitivity they need to serve patients in a community setting.

Students also learn about health promotion, illness prevention, primary medical care, and administration of the local health care systems.

In addition, a number of programs assign physicians to community service as a stopgap solution to the paucity of clinicians. This system needs to be replaced by health care models that offer incentives to physicians to remain in these underserved communities. Medical schools can offer an ongoing supply of students to provide rural communities with low-cost health care services. Such programs help meet the needs of underserved patients while providing medical students with important clinical experience and relevant research opportunities (Pulido, 1995). They also mark a return to the basic roots of medical education and its tradition of caring for the poor and needy.

THE BOON OF TECHNOLOGY

The term "telemedicine" includes a broad range of activities from the use of standard telephones and faxes to the use of highly complex systems, including computers, fiber optic cable, satellites, and other highly sophisticated equipment often needed to run various kinds of software (Mandil, 1998).

Telemedicine currently is used to facilitate clinical decision-making, as well as to exchange medical information (e.g., X-rays, electrocardiograms) to examine patients in real time who are located in geographically remote locations. Technology also is used to teleconference, teach, and gather epidemiological data. By using information systems to analyze the activities of professionals, academic health centers in Latin America will be able to tailor educational programs based on a realistic evaluation of student needs. As Venezuela and other Latin American countries design their educational platforms, they need to take into account the increasing presence of these new information and medical communications systems.

As one researcher has observed:

> It took two centuries to build the roads, rail lines, and seaports that form the backbone of Latin America's commercial infrastructure. By comparison, the region's information infrastructure seems to have appeared overnight—just ten years ago. (Constance, 1997).

Unfortunately, Latin America lacks a high-capacity telecommunications infrastructure with which to transmit data. As a result, telecommunications traffic originating in a given Latin American country must be routed through the United States via satellite or submarine cable.

DISTANCE LEARNING THROUGH INFORMATION TECHNOLOGY

To compete in the global village, Latin America and the Caribbean need to join the Information Technology (IT) society. The real challenge is to develop strategies and implement actions that will help countries make the transition from a communications network infrastructure aimed predominantly at voice telephony to high-tech, fully integrated networks with widely expanded functions.

The Intra-American Development Bank (IADB) developed its Informatics 2000 Initiative to encourage public and private sectors to implement significant IT applications by 2000. In 1999, a panel of technologists and scientists at the Presidential Summit in Santiago identified the necessary infrastructures, policies, and institutional developments for establishing extensive access to the Internet throughout the region.

With Informatics 2000 support, IADB is working with several countries, PAHO, and the Inter-American Telecommunication Commission (CITEL), the organization of telecommunications authorities in the hemisphere. A number of nongovernmental organizations and private companies also are contributing to this project.

Participants have formed a health task force consisting of regional experts and representatives from PAHO, WHO, other multilateral development agencies, and the IT industry. At a number of meetings held around the hemisphere, the task force analyzed current circumstances and made the following recommendations:

- Establish an Americas-Med Web site, to provide health care information.
- Set up Vi@Salud, a health care training and education program, under the leadership of the PAFAMS.
- Begin packaging applications and their financing for small hospitals and clinics.

- Install appropriate communications equipment and services to link health care facilities to information resources, expertise, training, and productivity tools.

As the reader may recall, in Latin America (as in other countries) distance education began as a school mail-order system, with class materials distributed by mail. Later many schools incorporated audio and video elements to supplement the printed materials. These methods all precluded a natural, personal interaction between teachers and students, a crucial element of the learning process. Now, thanks to satellite cable-based systems, schools are able to take advantage of low-cost electronic networks to transmit data to students far away. These technologies introduce the missing component of interactivity and distance education and are a competitive alternative to traditional methods of teaching.

Using digital TV and upgraded telephone systems, some academic health centers are designing continuing multimedia educational programs to satisfy the needs of professionals living in remote parts of the region. Digital TV not only has superb image quality and speed; it also vastly increases the number of channels available in each frequency band.* In addition, the enterprises carrying digital TV signals are able to satisfy the demand for entertainment while complying with their legal obligation to dedicate a certain percentage of their transmission time to cultural programming. Educational TV is an attractive way to meet this programming quota, since it also functions to lure new subscribers.

The new digital technologies provide distance education with a further advantage: they are available to the people who need it (either in the work place or at home), whenever they need it. Note, however, that the necessary communications resources for distance-learning pedagogic methodology are extremely specific. They differ highly from the widely accepted pedagogic methods seen in proximity education.

---

* The necessary communications resources for distance learning are extremely specific and differ greatly from the widely accepted methods seen in proximity education.

VI@SALUD: BREAKING NEW EDUCATIONAL GROUND

Vi@Salud's mission is to provide quality training at a distance for health service personnel, professionals and technicians through the use of real-time interactive techniques. It offers an electronic platform for disseminating information, telemedicine, education, health products, electronic commerce, and communication to Spanish-speaking health professionals throughout the Southern Hemisphere. Initially, its efforts are focused in Latin America.

The platform will include:

- Medical evidence (primary information from original sources)
- Structured courses and class materials
- Professional directory
- Services directory
- Pharmacopoeia directory
- Human resources directory

It is anticipated that the most immediate demand for Vi@Salud's services will come from the El Dorado market (110,000,000 people in a wealthy economic corridor from Chile and Argentina to Brazil), as well as from the decentralized state health services. We expect to encounter two types of students, at least initially: technical personnel from the state health directorates, and managerial and medical personnel from the hospitals and outpatient clinics of these states. In later stages, Vi@Salud's courses will target more specific medical specialties by updating relevant pathologies or offering training in new and more effective medical procedures. The project's goal is to teach 50,000 students by the end of the fifth year of service.

Vi@Salud will offer its educational products through both a Web site and a digital TV (satellite) channel. Each 12-week course will consist of 12 lectures, offered in conjunction with 24 hours of supervised work. During the initial phase, this project will be centered in Venezuela. Once underway, it will be expanded to serve other countries, including Argentina, Brazil, Colombia, Costa Rica, Chile, Haiti, and Mexico.

By providing training to health care professionals throughout Latin America and the Caribbean, Vi@Salud serves as an example of the type of program that will support ongoing reforms in health services. It also improves the organization and management of public health services at both the primary and secondary levels of health care. By promoting interactions among health care professionals throughout Latin America, it also alleviates the chronic problem of professional isolation and reduces the existing gaps in technology and quality of care.

THE FUTURE OF MEDICAL EDUCATION

Distance education enhances the quality of health care while lowering costs and fosters community continuing education and volunteerism. By maintaining basic health records, it lays the groundwork for more comprehensive databases that, in turn, can serve as an infrastructure for social welfare reforms.

Providing medical education and services to the underserved continues to be a challenge throughout the hemisphere. Obtaining political endorsement for distance education should come with relative ease.

REFERENCES

The American Assembly. 1999. *The future of the western hemisphere: US National Interests.* New York, NY: Columbia University.

Bankowski Z and Mejia A. 1987. *Health Manpower Out of Balance: Conflicts and Prospects: Proceedings of the XXth CIOMS Round Table Conference Acapulco Mexico, 7-12 Sept. 1987.* Albany, NY: World Health Organization.

Burki SH and Perry GE. 1998. *Beyond the Washington Consensus: Institutions Matter.* (World Bank Latin American and Caribbean Studies) Washington, DC: The World Bank.

Centro Latinamericano de Demografia, Celade. 1993. *Población, equidad y transformación productiva.* Santiago de Chile: CEPAL.

Constance P. 1997. Who is building the data highways? *IDB America.*

Evans JR. 1981. *Measurement and Management in Medicine and Health Services: Training Needs and Opportunities.* New York, NY: The Rockefeller Foundation.

Federacion Panamericana de Asociaciones de Facultades y Escuelas de Medicina. 1990. *Educación Médica en las Américas: El reto de los años '90.* (Informe final del Proyecto EMA)

Caracas, Venezuela: FEPAFEM.

Field M. 1996. *Telemedicine: A Guide to Assessing Telecommunications in Health Care.* Washington, DC: National Academy Press.

Landes D. 1998. *The Wealth and Poverty of Nations.* London: Little, Brown and Co.

Mandil S. 1998. TeleHealth. What is it? Will it propel cross-border trade in health services in international trade? In *Health Services: A Development Perspective.* S. Zarrilli and C. Kinnon, eds. Geneva, Switzerland: WHO, UN Conference on Trade and Development.

Martini C. 1992. Calidad y costo de la atención médica. *Boletín de la Academia Nacional de Medicina de Buenos Aires,* Suppl. 4, 67-72.

McGuire CH. 1994. An overview of medical education in the late twentieth century. In *Sociedad y Estratificación: Método Graffar-Méndez Castellano,* AW Sajid, CH McGuire, CH Mendez, MC Mendez, eds.. Caracas, Venezuela: Fundacredesa.

McKinsey Global Institute. 1994. *Latin American Productivity.* Washington, DC: McKinsey & Company.

Mendez CH, Mendez MC. 1994. *Sociedad y Estratificación: Método Graffar-Méndez Castellano.* Caracas, Venezuela: Fundacredesa.

Mosbacher, R. 1999. Latin America in the next millennium. *World Energy,* 2(2):56-59.

Nash, D. 1993. *Future Practice Alternatives in Medicine.* New York, NY: Igaku-Shoin Medical Publishers.

Pan American Health Organization. 1998. I*nformation Systems and Information Technology in Health.* Washington, DC: PAHO/OPS Scientific Publication.

Panamericana de Asociaciones de Facultades y Escuelas de Medicina. *1995 Annual Report.* Caracas, Venezuela: PAFAMS.

Patiño, JF. 1997. *Why PAFAMS? An International Challenge and An Opportunity of Collaborative Action.* Bogotá, Colombia: PAFAMS.

—— 1989. Strategies for developing innovative programs in international medical education: A viewpoint from Latin America, *Academic Medicine,* 64:17-22.

—— 1995. Strengthening health care infrastructure. In *Challenges For Leadership in Latin America: Socioeconomic Policies and Political Institutions: The Ninth NOMOS Seminar,* MR Tomz, ed. Cambridge, MA: Harvard University Press.

—— 1996. Medical practice and medical education in Latin America, strategies for change. *Education for Health,* 9(3):289-306.

Sajid AW, McGuire CH, Veach RM. 1994. *International Handbook of Medcal Education.* Westport, CT: Greenwood Publishing Group.

Shapiro A. 1999. The Internet. Foreign Policy, Summer 115.

Solari, A., ed. 1985. *Managed Prepaid Health Care in Latin America and the Caribbean: A Critical Assessment.* Washington, DC: US Agency for International Development, Bureau for Latin America and the Caribbean.

Telcordia Technologies (formerly Bellcore). 1998. *White Paper on Investment Priorities for the Information Infrastructure in Latin America and the Caribbean.* San Diego, CA: Science Applications International Corporation.

Thorp, R. 1998. *Progress, Poverty and Exclusion; An Economic History of Latin America in the 20th Century.* Washington, DC: The John Hopkins University Press and the Inter American Development Bank.

——1993. *Hacia Una Política Social Efectiva en Venezuela: Comunicación, Creación de Consenso y Reforma.* Washington, DC: Banco Interamericano de Desarrollo.

Vi@Salud, 1998. FEPAFEM-PAFAMS-Fundacion Venezolana Para la Salud. Caracas, Venezuela: FEPAFEM/PAFAMS.

The World Bank. 1993. *World Development Report: Investing in Health.* New York, NY: Oxford University Press.

——— 1995. *World Development Report: Workers in an Integrating World.* New York, NY: Oxford University Press.

——— 1998/99. *World Development Report: Knowledge for Development.* New York, NY: Oxford University Press.

ENHANCING EDUCAITONAL MISSIONS THROUGH INITIATIVES ABROAD

12. *Educating Tomorrow's Practitioners*

LOUIS W. SULLIVAN

THE MOREHOUSE SCHOOL OF MEDICINE (MSM) began operations in 1978. In 1984, thanks to a grant from the U.S. Agency for International Development (USAID), MSM offered its first international programs. Since then, Morehouse has continued to carry out its international mission in a variety of ways. First, we hired a vice president of sponsored programs to oversee international activities. This office negotiates with the dean and vice president of academic affairs to hire faculty and staff for specific programs overseas. Most of the programs are USAID-supported and administered in partnership with other organizations, such as the Tulane School of Tropical Medicine and Public Health, the Johns Hopkins School of Hygiene and Public Health, and the American International Health Alliance (AIHA).

MSM's international programs range widely in duration and scope, from 4-week faculty development courses for teachers from schools in sub-Saharan Africa, to a 5-year program in health system development for AIDS education and prevention in Zambia. The programs cover a variety of sites and purposes, including:

- Strengthening medical library programs in Tbilisi, Republic of Georgia.
- Developing a School of Public Health in Senegal, in association with Tulane University.
- Working with traditional healers in Senegal to expand the network of health educators for that country.

TRAINING BLACK HEALTH PROFESSIONALS IN SOUTH AFRICA

A MSM program developed and implemented in conjunction with The Johns Hopkins University trains nurse-midwives with a focus on AIDS education and prevention. Our family medicine curricular development programs draw faculty from Liberia, Zimbabwe, Sudan, and Uganda, but we do more than import international teachers. Over the years, Morehouse students have taken elective courses in Zimbabwe, Botswana, Nigeria, and Senegal.

This kind of internationalism has been an integral part of the Morehouse experience for over 15 years. In 1985, Joy Kaiser and her husband, Herb, a retired U.S. foreign service officer, formed an organization called Medical Education for South African Blacks (MESAB) to train health professionals for that country. At the time of its independence from apartheid, South Africa had only 700 black physicians in a nation of some 40 million people. As late as 1985, South Africa had only two black board-certified psychiatrists, six cardiac surgeons, and four neurologists. The numbers of black practitioners in the other health care specialties were equally sparse.

When MSM began its international programs, South Africa was a country of great paradoxes. To this day, high-quality health care is readily available to those South Africans who are white, wealthy, and live in urban areas, but if one is black, poor, or from a rural area, health services are often inadequate or even nonexistent. Many black communities still have no health services whatsoever.

In the mid-1980s, South African universities began to open their doors to nonwhite students. At last, blacks were admitted to these schools, but scholarship funds were still virtually unavailable. Since the average black South African family income was less than $500 per year, and medical school tuition (excluding room and board) was approximately $5,000, offering admission to blacks without providing scholarship support was no more than an empty gesture. MESAB stepped in to fill the financial void by raising funds for scholarships.

MESAB's Board of Trustees raises funds in both the United States and South Africa, although more than 90 percent of the funds come from the United States. I am honored to serve as the current chair of MESAB. In South Africa, we have an on-site board that dispenses funds to scholarship recipients. This board currently is chaired by Dr. Intado Mafana, who served as the personal physician to the former President of South Africa, Nelson Mandela.

Over the years, MESAB has supported 3,000 black South African students in the fields of medicine, dentistry, pharmacy, veterinary medicine, medical technology, nurse-midwifery, audiology, speech therapy, and other areas. Currently, MESAB supports some 700 students a year. Our primary fund-raising event is an annual dinner. The MESAB benefit dinner in New York City on February 28, 2000, honored Nelson Mandela for his leadership role in helping South Africa break the bonds of apartheid.

Today, MESAB's annual budget is approximately three million dollars. Though this is a modest sum, MESAB has become the largest source of private, nongovernmental scholarship support for blacks in South Africa. It is one of Morehouse's most successful international programs, and certainly one in which we take great pride.

CONTROLLING AIDS IN SUB-SAHARAN AFRICA

In addition to MESAB, Morehouse has developed another program called "Secure the Future." Funded by Bristol-Myers Squibb, it is offered in conjunction with the Baylor School of Medicine and the Harvard Medical School's AIDS Project. Secure the Future focuses on stopping fetal transmission of HIV in five sub-Saharan nations, all with an exceptionally high incidence of HIV/AIDS: South Africa, Botswana, Namibia, Lesotho, and

Swaziland. Of the 33 million people around the world currently infected with HIV, 22 million are located in sub-Saharan Africa. In many of these countries, the incidence of HIV infection within a single village is 40 to 45 percent of all adults of reproductive age.

Because HIV infection in Southern Africa poses a serious global health threat, Bristol-Myers Squibb has committed one hundred million dollars to the Secure the Future program. Through Secure the Future, health care practitioners have access to the best therapies available, whether the products are made by Bristol-Myers Squibb or another company. It is our sincere hope that other corporations will follow Bristol-Myers Squibb in funding this important effort to stop transmission of the HIV virus in areas where the disease has become most rampant.

WHY DEVELOP INTERNATIONAL PROGRAMS?

What is Morehouse's rationale for developing such international programs? First, we are committed to improving the quality and accessibility of health services in poor and developing countries, particularly in sub-Saharan Africa. Second, we are helping to train the kind of health care workforce that these countries so desperately need. Third, we are expanding the range of educational experiences for our students. Fourth, we are developing new research opportunities. For instance, Morehouse researchers are conducting comparisons of the health problems of African Americans versus those problems among Africans. They are discovering significant differences in the incidence of heart disease, prostate cancer, and cervical cancer.

Finally, Morehouse sponsors these international programs because they serve an important social purpose on a global scale. Through MESAB, we are helping develop a black middle class in South Africa. This, in turn, strengthens that country's commitment to democratic principles and basic human rights. It will support and stabilize social reforms in this still-new democracy.

Although reforms are also taking place in other African countries such as Mali, Senegal, Nigeria, Tanzania, and Namibia, unfortunately, most people in the United States never hear about them. Morehouse's international programs serve to encourage economic investments in these developing countries, fostering economic stability and job development.

What are the outcomes of Morehouse's efforts over the past two decades? We have helped to establish one school of public health in Senegal, and another in South Africa at the Medical University of South Africa. We have provided elective clinical experiences for more than fifty of our students, who uniformly return to Morehouse enthused about their experiences. Our international programs often give medical students more opportunities to assist in deliveries or surgeries than in U.S. universities. These programs also offer faculty members very special sorts of clinical experience.

Indicative of the respect that South Africans themselves have for the MESAB program is the selection by the country's new President, Thabo Mbeki, of a MESAB graduate, Dr. David Indaba, as his personal physician. Dr. Indaba also holds a position in the South African Ministry of Health, where he is overseeing the development of telecommunication systems to connect all of South Africa's eight medical schools.

It is clear, then, that Morehouse's international health care programs foster health and well-being in the developing world, especially in South Africa; they promote the basic humanitarian principles undergirding the whole profession of medicine; and they give participating students and faculty members a broader perspective of our world and important insight into the phenomenon of global health.

MORE THAN A GOOD CAUSE

Because the United States is blessed with rich opportunities and many smoothly functioning systems, we have an ethical responsibility to assist other countries that need and invite our help. This is not just good social policy; it is good political and economic policy. We live in a global environment, and what one country does affects all the others.

However, before other academic institutions rush out to implement their own international health care programs, let me offer several cautions. First, working with developing countries should be approached as a partnership. We in the United States have much to share, but we also have much to learn. Our colleagues in developing countries expect and deserve to be treated with respect and understanding. They are working with us as equals.

The second caution is that program developers need to take the time to learn the culture of the country where they will be working, and respect that culture. U.S. schools will end up with a more successful and enduring program by educating themselves in this way.

Third, be prepared for some delays or setbacks due to local customs and, certainly due to local politics. Our colleagues in developing countries want our help and our participation, but they want it on their terms. Understanding and even expecting this will enable program administrators to deal better with the delays or complications that are bound to arise along the way.

Now that the era of the Cold War is behind us, our nation needs to invest more of its human and material resources in programs that support the health and socioeconomic development of poor nations around the world. It is not only the right thing to do; it is also the smart thing to do.

13. Doing Well by Doing Good

Virginia D. McGill

ILAC has been a time of learning. I learned Spanish. I learned how to cut a coconut with a peso. I learned about medicine and teamwork. I learned that children, no matter what race, love baseball and are ticklish. I learned how two-thirds of the world lives, and was able to experience a small part of their world.

—Tom Rangitsch,
3rd-year medical student, Institute for Latin American Concern
1999 Summer Program

SINCE 1975, STUDENTS AND FACULTY FROM CREIGHTON University and other educational institutions have been traveling to the Dominican Republic with the Institute for Latin American Concern (ILAC) programs to help thousands of Dominican people learn more about basic health care, occupational and physical therapy, hygiene, and injury and disease prevention. ILAC participants often are the only source of health care, education, and assistance available to farming communities in remote mountain villages and to Dominicans in Santiago's economically disadvantaged neighborhoods.

Perhaps even more valuable than the direct health care services that the ILAC program offers are the unique educational opportunities they provide for North American participants. ILAC's summer health care, occupational therapy, and physical therapy programs, and its semester-abroad programs all offer participants experience with developing practical solutions to health maintenance challenges to underserved populations. Students also gain awareness of global health issues while they grow personally, professionally, and spiritually. And during the personal experience of living and working with the Dominican people, participants develop close relationships with their Dominican hosts. Furthermore, ILAC's immersion programs enhance Creighton University's mission to educate students broadly, with a view to their intellectual growth, social and physical development, aesthetic appreciation, and spiritual enrichment. Programs coordinated through ILAC embrace Creighton's core values, which underscore service to others, the importance of family life, the inalienable worth of each individual, and an appreciation of ethnic and cultural diversity.

TWENTY-FIVE YEARS OF COMMUNITY SERVICE

ILAC's commitment to the Dominican people has grown dramatically over the past two and a half decades. What began as a consciousness-raising program for a small team of concerned participants has evolved into a program encompassing a variety of year-round programs. ILAC now involves hundreds of volunteers from Creighton and other North American academic institutions, as well as from numerous organizations within the Dominican Republic. Much of this work is coordinated through the ILAC/Creighton Centro de Educacion para la Salud Integral, or Center for Integral Health.

The ILAC Centro, an eight-building facility located on several acres of land outside Santiago, represents Creighton's permanent commitment to addressing the educational and health care needs of the Dominican people. Established and incorporated as a nonprofit Dominican institution through Creighton University, the ILAC Centro also serves as an academic campus and home for the university's varied endeavors in the Dominican Republic. Under the direction of ILAC's founder and executive director, Fr. Ernesto

Travieso, the Centro employs 22 full-time Dominican administrators and staff members.

ILAC originated in 1972 at Regis College in Toronto, Canada, as an immersion program for Jesuit seminarians seeking to experience the complexities of living in a developing country. Fr. Travieso, a Jesuit priest, developed the program through which young Jesuits spent a summer living with Dominican families learning Spanish, observing the daily activities of the Dominican people, and reflecting upon their experiences.

The program gave participants a broader understanding of global interconnectedness and responsibility. Each seminarian lived with a Dominican family. This form of cultural immersion was central to the program's success because it provided natural opportunities for genuine connections and personal exchanges between the students and their hosts. A typical day might find the students washing clothes in the river with their families, harvesting coffee, readying family meals over wood-burning stoves, and attending Spanish-language classes.

In 1975, Fr. Travieso began working at Creighton University as chaplain of the medical school and a faculty member in the College of Arts and Sciences. This relocation forged a link between the existing Jesuit student program and available resources at Creighton. Soon, the program grew beyond the initial vision of its founder. In 1977, a team of faculty members and students from Creighton's dental, medical, nursing, pharmacy, and undergraduate schools joined Jesuit seminarians taking part in the ILAC program.

The program's expansion to include students and faculty members from the health sciences schools changed the character of ILAC dramatically. Rather than remaining solely an immersion experience, ILAC expanded into a health care program as participants from Creighton secured medicines and provided health care and educational services for the Dominican people. No longer relying solely on the hospitality and generosity of the Dominican host families, Creighton now was able to give back to those communities by directly addressing some of their most important health issues.

HELPING TO MEET A DESPERATE NEED

In the late 1970s, the Dominican Republic faced monumental obstacles in attaining reasonable health care and living standards for the majority of its population. Most Dominicans lived in conditions of material poverty, disease, poor sanitation, and unemployment. They lacked ample food, water, shelter, and other necessities. By adding a health care and educational component to the ILAC experience, Creighton was able, at least in part, to help the Dominican Republic surmount some of its domestic problems.

The need for health care and education was (and continues to be) enormous throughout the Caribbean. ILAC, therefore, chose to concentrate on providing its health care and educational services to economically disadvantaged families in the most remote farming regions, or campos, generally beyond the reach of the existing government health programs. In keeping with the initial focus on immersion and reflection, the program offered half-day clinics after which participants had ample time to discuss their experiences with one another, interact with their host communities, and become better acquainted with their Dominican families.

Dominican involvement in the ILAC program also changed dramatically when the health care component was added. To assist teams in making the transition from an immersion experience to a program combining immersion with service, it was imperative that Dominican leaders identify the needs of their local communities. To that end, ILAC linked with an existing health promotion program, the Cooperadores de la Salud (Health Partners). Creighton assumed all financial responsibility for the program's continued development, staffing, and expansion. As an established initiative that was organized and led by Dominicans, the cooperadores program provided vital, collaborative connections between Creighton, ILAC, and the Dominican Republic.

EMPOWERING PEOPLE TO HELP THEMSELVES

Through the cooperadores program, Dominican women and men are selected by their local campo communities to receive 4 weeks of intensive health care education at the ILAC Centro. Cooperadores then go back to their communities to use what they have learned. They return monthly to the Centro for further training. This continuing training encompasses both health education and disease prevention. It also gives the cooperadores an opportunity to share health-related information with their colleagues from other communities. Additionally, ILAC conducts ongoing cooperadore education through weekly radio broadcasts on health-related topics. These broadcasts not only promote the cooperadores' continuing education, but also enable program participants to relay important health information from one remote community to another.

Currently, over 200 cooperadores have been trained by ILAC and are volunteering in over 300 rural communities. They work in immunization, disease prevention, health education, and basic public health improvement. Cooperadores also serve a triage function, ensuring that members of rural communities in most urgent need receive the care they need at a more central location. They also work diligently to help farming families obtain health care services that otherwise could not be found, afforded, or accessed.

Cooperadores provide an important link between ILAC summer teams and the campos. During the summer program, six teams of health science students, faculty members, dentists, physicians, and registered nurses travel to various rural campos where cooperadores serve as leaders. Based on the cooperadores' assessment of campo needs, teams are set up to establish makeshift dental and medical clinics in rural sites located in the Dominican Republic's Central Mountain Range and on the Dominican-Haitian border. These clinics provide care for over 6,000 Dominicans and Haitians each summer. The ILAC summer program teams work in disease treatment, prevention, and education. This is a valuable supplement to the year-round work conducted in these campos by Cooperadores de la Salud.

In 1991, in a commitment to providing additional health outreach to the campos, Creighton, ILAC, and Cooperadores de la Salud established the VIDAS program (Volunteers for Action and Service). Under the leadership of the cooperadores in the campos where ILAC has long-standing relationships, VIDAS participants construct permanent clinics in campo communities without access to health facilities. Numerous ILAC alumni volunteers, along with local Dominican health care professionals, assist the cooperadores in staffing these clinics full time.

ADDING OCCUPATIONAL AND PHYSICAL THERAPY AND EYE CARE

In 1991, ILAC formed a committee consisting of one Creighton occupational therapy graduate, one summer program alumnus, and several cooperadores to assess the potential benefit of adding an occupational therapy component to the summer program. The assessment noted that, while on-site therapy and education was valuable, administration would be difficult because of the remote location of the campos, scattered housing, and the relatively small number of inhabitants in these regions. In addition, an increased number of farming families were being forced to move to larger cities in search of employment due to dwindling campo economics and the decline in crop sales. Following months of dialogue with the cooperadores, other campo leaders, and Dominican leaders in Santiago health care facilities, ILAC outlined a program that would offer occupational therapy services to campo families forced to migrate to Santiago. Up to this point, no occupational therapists had been trained or were working in the Dominican Republic.

In 1993, ILAC's first team of occupational therapy students and professionals began a month-long, city-based experience of service, immersion, and reflection. The team lived at the ILAC Centro campus and offered therapy to people at a variety of Santiago sites. They included a meningitis clinic, a children's hospital, a home for the elderly, a rehabilitation agency, and a school for children with special needs.

Cooperadores taught classes focusing on educational terminology specific to occupational therapy. In keeping with ILAC's initial immersion focus, participants were assigned host families and spent part of each day organizing children's games, assisting in meal preparations, and improving their Spanish by conversing and interacting with their Dominican hosts.

In 1996, Creighton and ILAC utilized the occupational therapy program as a model for a physical therapy program. This program, again based out of the ILAC Centro in Santiago and relying on the organizational skills of the Cooperadores, offered avenues for physical therapy students to provide care and continuing education at the same hospitals and facilities staffed by the occupational therapy participants. This month-long rotation provides service to the Dominicans while it gives North American participants an opportunity for personal and professional growth. As with the other ILAC programs, such growth is made possible through the immersion experience of living and working in a developing country.

Cooperadores also served as integral links in developing ILAC's eye program. Begun in 1995 and based out of the ILAC Centro, the eye care program was organized by two Creighton alumni associated with the New York Eye and Ear Infirmary. It uses the ILAC Centro and local Santiago hospitals to provide eye care for over 800 Dominican patients, all from campo regions, each year. Cooperadores identify, select, prepare, and provide follow-up care for patients who receive treatment for glaucoma, cataracts, strabismus, congenital eye deformities, eye infections, acquired trauma, and eyelid tumors.

EXPANDING THE CURRICULUM

Capitalizing on the success of ILAC's health care programs and the solid relationships that ILAC has developed with the Dominican people over a quarter century, Creighton's College of Arts and Sciences began a Dominican Republic semester-abroad program in 1992. Through this program, undergraduate students enroll in 15 hours of academic courses at the ILAC Centro. While there, they interact with Dominican families, travel to campos with cooperadores, and commit themselves to service work within the campos and the health care facilities served by the occupational and physical therapy programs. The same immersion opportunities for learning about the Dominican culture, language, and lifestyle are integral components of the semester-abroad program.

In the fall of 1994, the Creighton College of Business Administration began its own semester abroad program, also based at the ILAC Centro, which emphasizes international business experience. It provides business students with the same kind of campo and health care service opportunities offered to Arts and Sciences students.

All ILAC and Creighton programs respond in various ways to the needs of the economically disadvantaged people of the Dominican Republic, an outgrowth of both ILAC's and Creighton University's long-standing commitment to social justice. The expansion of these programs has fostered an increased interest in international affairs at Creighton. It also has inspired many health science and undergraduate students to enroll in ILAC programs. Well over one-half of the students who have taken part in ILAC programs return to the Dominican Republic every year regularly or as full-time practitioners: dentists, occupational therapists, physical therapists, registered nurses, pharmacists, and physicians.

Numerous faculty members and other professionals also return (some over a dozen times) to take part in ILAC programs, noting that they provide powerful cultural and professional experiences that remind them why they entered the health care profession in the first place.

14. Expanding Access to Quality Care Abroad

STEVEN J. THOMPSON

THE FORCES DRIVING THE GLOBALIZATION OF HEALTH care today can be divided into two distinct areas: internal and external. Issues internal to the health care system of the United States are driving organizations to look to other sources of revenue. The Balanced Budget Act of 1997 and U.S. health-care payer behavior have both reinforced the need to search outside the United States for other avenues of income. External factors include a worldwide increase in people's desire to seek high-quality health care. The increasing availability of information from various sources, including the Internet, has raised people's awareness of disparities in the quality of health care services. Another external factor is the emergence of private insurance programs in many developing countries. Additionally, multinational corporations and their employees throughout the world are demanding access to quality health care as a benefit before accepting out-of-country postings.

In response to these factors, as well as to fulfill the university's desire to expand its role internationally, Johns Hopkins International, L.L.C., was formed. This organization was established to bring the excellence of Johns Hopkins Medicine to the world. Traditionally, the faculty members at The Johns Hopkins University have played an important role in advancing health care throughout the world. In the past, this was driven primarily by those Hopkins faculty members who are based in Baltimore. The mission of Johns Hopkins International now is to develop, establish, and operate business ventures that promote the goals of the tripartite mission of Johns Hopkins Medicine: excellence in research, education, and clinical care.

To this end, Johns Hopkins International has been charged with several goals:

1. To continue developing, refining, and implementing the international strategy for Johns Hopkins Medicine.
2. To enter into international agreements on behalf of Johns Hopkins Medicine.
3. To facilitate and coordinate all international activities for Johns Hopkins Medicine

Beyond these goals, Johns Hopkins International was also established to provide an additional layer of control for Johns Hopkins Medicine. This organization was established as a vehicle for limiting tax exposure and liability. It was also created as an organization to facilitate foreign business development.

Johns Hopkins International continues to direct patients to Johns Hopkins in Baltimore whenever appropriate. It also acts as a resource on all international matters for members of the faculty, staff, and administration of Johns Hopkins Medicine, and serves as the liaison with other Johns Hopkins University divisions.

Traditionally, Johns Hopkins Medicine's international activities have focused on recruiting patients to come to Baltimore to obtain medical care. This has been viewed as the last source of full-pay patients. We have identified a significant population throughout the world of potential patients who have the means and the desire to travel for health care. Johns Hopkins International seeks to capitalize on the Johns Hopkins name and reputation. The strategic vision for the new organization includes expanding the Johns Hopkins service community well beyond the university's traditional reach.

This is consistent with the Johns Hopkins goal to become a global university. In addition, technology (telemedicine, the Internet, etc.) further facilitates this global expansion of medical services.

A FIVEFOLD FOCUS

Johns Hopkins International is focusing its activities in on five distinct areas within the international health services area as follows:

1. The international patient services program at Johns Hopkins International provides traditional services, such as translating a patient's medical records and documents before he or she obtains services. Johns Hopkins International also schedules and coordinates medical appointments and helps patients meet hospital admission requirements. It provides a second opinion and consultation service to referring physicians throughout the world. The office also arranges transportation and housing for patients and families and provides interpretation services during all phases of medical treatment.

2. The telemedicine utility provider at Johns Hopkins International serves all departments and divisions of Johns Hopkins Medicine with computer hardware, software, and staffing to coordinate all aspects of telemedical services. This includes telepathology, teleradiology, and a second-opinion service, as well as teleconsultation with live video presentation. The technology used to convey this medical information ranges from traditional telephonic and facsimile service to the more advanced live video links.

3. Johns Hopkins International offers a program of health care consultation services that includes:
    - Clinical program assessment, planning, and development.
    - Monitoring of quality assurance systems (the Joint Committee on Accreditation of Healthcare Organizations accreditation standards).
    - Strategic planning.
    - Monitoring of clinical outcomes.
    - Financial management.
    - Marketing of health care services.

In addition to these areas, the health care consultation team assesses staffing needs and offers advice regarding the application of information technology to health care facilities and clinical programs.

On a consulting basis, Johns Hopkins International also helps plan facilities, either for a defined term or on an open-ended basis. The organization's experience as an international health care consultant recently led to several opportunities in health care facility management. Many of these opportunities are currently under review.

4. Johns Hopkins International functions as the marketing arm for the university's continuing medical education (CME) program. In addition to traditional CME courses and seminars held throughout the United States, the organization offers customized programs that are developed for a particular client or organization. Johns Hopkins International also produces print and electronic publications for physicians around the world, and physicians may take advantage of the program's weekly "grand rounds" held on the Internet.

5. Johns Hopkins International is developing health care facilities throughout the world, using a hub-and-spoke model. These facilities will enable Hopkins Medicine practitioners to serve in various clinical settings around the world, where they can also explore opportunities to implement research, training/education, and patient-care programs. The first of these facilities was developed in Singapore; it serves as the hub with spokes reaching out to Southeast Asia.

A NEW VENTURE IN SINGAPORE

In 1998, after meeting with the government of Singapore and other local health care partners within Singapore, Johns Hopkins established two distinct health care entities in Singapore. Johns Hopkins Singapore, built to house all research and educational programs, is wholly owned by Johns Hopkins International and its parent, the University and Health System. Johns Hopkins Singapore Clinical Services is the clinical-service provider. Ultimately, the clinical services program will become the vehicle through which we will develop a full-fledged, multispecialty health care facility in Singapore. This facility is owned by Johns Hopkins International and other Singapore partners.

The clinical services organization was established to focus on tertiary and quaternary care in various specialties. In Phase I, a medical oncology program is being expanded to include hematologic malignancies and offer radiation oncology capabilities. The long-term plan is to establish a multi-specialty clinical facility; in the meantime, clinical program expansion is being guided by regional health care needs.

The clinical facility is located in the Kent Ridge Wing of the National University Hospital. A new facility, it had been unoccupied and was made available to Johns Hopkins through lease arrangements with the National University Hospital and other external providers. Additionally, we plan to build an outpatient facility in the central commercial district of Singapore. To date, approximately 50 percent of the patients seeking services at this facility are from Singapore. The remainder come from a variety of countries throughout the region, including Malaysia, Indonesia, Bangladesh, Sri Lanka, Thailand, Myanmar, and the Philippines.

The educational programs offered at Johns Hopkins Singapore are provided in collaboration with the National University. The collaboration focuses on making educational programs available to the entire region. These programs include:

- Undergraduate medical education
- Specialty training programs
- Research training programs
- Clinical training programs
- Joint PhD program
- Postdoctoral fellowship training, both basic and applied research
- Continuing medical education programs in the region

The Johns Hopkins Singapore research programs are funded by external organizations at approximately $US7 million per year. This research is carried out in two facilities, one with approximately 40,000 square feet of wet lab space and another with 10,000 square feet of dry lab and administrative space. The focus of the research programs in Singapore can be categorized as transnational research leading to the development of commercially viable products and other spinoff business opportunities. Other research focuses on work in a drug development unit and a clinical trials program. Individual research projects are awarded funding through a competitive peer-review process. Particular consideration is given to projects dealing with health matters important to the peoples in the region. To date, 10 projects have been funded and are underway, including research into acute-angle glaucoma, a study of the genetics of cranial facial defects, and an examination of those types of cancer that are prevalent in the Singapore region, such as nasopharyngeal and hepatic cancer.

Through its exclusive ownership of Johns Hopkins Singapore, Johns Hopkins retains significant control over the quality of medical services and the selection of practicing physicians. It also maintains control over use of the Hopkins name. Johns Hopkins Medicine, through Johns Hopkins International, controls the Clinical Services Board by approving the board's membership and holding the chairman's position.

In sum, Johns Hopkins Medicine has created a novel vehicle for effectively positioning itself as a leader in the globalization of health care. Johns Hopkins International will be the avenue through which Johns Hopkins Medicine can achieve its mission—pursuing excellence in patient care, research, and education—by offering high-quality health care services to the peoples of the world.